de Gruyter Studies in Organization 46
International Management Research

de Gruyter Studies in Organization
International Management, Organization and Policy Analysis

An international and interdisciplinary book series from de Gruyter presenting comprehensive research on aspects of international management, organization studies and comparative public policy.
It covers cross-cultural and cross-national studies of topics such as:
– management; organizations; public policy, and/or their inter-relation
– industry and regulatory policies
– business-government relations
– international organizations
– comparative institutional frameworks.

While each book in the series ideally has a comparative empirical focus, specific national studies of a general theoretical, substantive or regional interest which relate to the development of cross-cultural and comparative theory are also encouraged.
The series is designed to stimulate and encourage the exchange of ideas across linguistic, national and cultural traditions of analysis, between academic researchers, practitioners and policy makers, and between disciplinary specialisms.
The volumes present theoretical work, empirical studies, translations and 'state-of-the-art' surveys. The *international* aspects of the series are uppermost: there is a strong commitment to work which crosses and opens boundaries.

Editor:

Prof. Stewart R. Clegg, University of St. Andrews, Dept. of Management, St. Andrews, Scotland, U.K.

Advisory Board:

Prof. Nancy J. Adler, McGill University, Dept. of Management, Montreal, Quebec, Canada
Prof. Richard Hall, State University of New York at Albany, Dept. of Sociology, Albany, New York, USA
Prof. Gary Hamilton, University of California, Dept. of Sociology, Davis, California, USA
Prof. Geert Hofstede, University of Limburg, Maastricht, The Netherlands
Prof. Pradip N. Khandwalla, Indian Institute of Management, Vastrapur, Ahmedabad, India
Prof. Surendra Munshi, Sociology Group, Indian Institute of Management, Calcutta, India
Prof. Gordon Redding, University of Hong Kong, Dept. of Management Studies, Hong Kong

International Management Research

Looking to the Future

Edited by
Durhane Wong-Rieger and Fritz Rieger

Walter de Gruyter · Berlin · New York 1993

Durhane Wong-Rieger
Associate Professor of Psychology, University of Windsor, Windsor, Ontario, Canada
Fritz Rieger
Associate Professor of Management, University of Windsor, Windsor, Ontario, Canada

With 2 figures and 7 tables

∞ Printed on acid-free paper which falls within the guidelines of the ANSI to ensure permanence and durability.

Library of Congress Cataloging-in-Publication Data

International management research : looking to the future / edited by Durhane Wong-Rieger, Fritz Rieger.
   p. cm. – – (De Gruyter studies in organization : 46)
Papers from a conference entitled: "Research for relevance in international management" held in June 1988 and hosted by the University of Windsor in Ontario, Canada.
Includes bibliographical references.
ISBN 3–11–013378–4
  1. Management – Research – International cooperation – Congresses.
  2. Personnel management – Research – International cooperation – Congresses.
  3. International business enterprises – Management – Research – Congresses.
I. Wong-Rieger, Durhane, 1950– II. Rieger, Fritz, 1944– III. Series.
HD30.4.I58 1993
658'.0072 – dc20   92-45752

Die Deutsche Bibliothek – Cataloging-in-Publication Data

International management research : looking to the future / ed. by Durhane Wong-Rieger ; Fritz Rieger. – Berlin ; New York : de Gruyter, 1993
(De Gruyter studies in organization ; 46)
ISBN 3–11–013378–4
NE: Wong-Rieger, Durhane [Hrsg.]; GT

Converted by: Frohberg GmbH, Freigericht – Printing: Gerike GmbH, Berlin – Binding: Lüderitz & Bauer-GmbH, Berlin – Cover Design: Johannes Rother, Berlin

Preface

In June 1988, fifty leading international management researchers and a number of practitioners were invited to participate in a conference entitled "Research for Relevance in International Management". It was hosted by the University of Windsor, in Ontario, Canada. The mission, as set forth before the participants, was to envision the directions which international management research should take if it were to be useful to organizations in the 1990's and beyond. In order to achieve this mission, it was the organizers' perception that a format which reversed the usually high ratio of formal presentations to more informal "coffee-break discussion" was necessary. Thus presentations were limited to six keynote addresses, and the remainder of the time was devoted to small workshop sessions.

The conference convened, appropriately enough, in facilities situated on the Detroit River which is part of the international border separating the United States from Canada. The two countries were on the brink of signing a hotly debated Free Trade Agreement and the site itself was the headquarters of a very recent international merger between Hiram Walker Gooderham Worts, a Canadian distilling and beverage company and Allied-Lyons, a British food services conglomerate.

In the opening address, David Ricks, then editor of the Journal of International Business Studies (JIBS), recaptured what he considered to be the significant advances made in the field of International Management (IM) research over the past decade. He then presented an overview of a survey conducted specifically for the conference in which he had polled members of the International Management Division of the Academy of Management for their suggestions as to the directions in which IM research ought to be going.

Following this address, six leading researchers in the field of International Management (Nancy Adler, Yves Doz, Steve Kobrin, Dick Peterson, Gordon Redding and Rosalie Tung), offered their perspectives on the critical issues which would be driving international business and international management research through the 1990's. Each then led a workshop group which included some equally eminent researchers, a few newer IM faculty members, several practitioners (executives and consultants) and several doctoral student delegates. The six groups each met twice. Their objectives in the first workshop were to share ideas about the future context of international business and to define the directions which they felt IM research would need to take in order to be relevant to these contexts. This was followed by a plenary session where the conclusions from these workshops were presented and discussed further. The plenary closed with a provocative commentary from Henry Mintzberg.

At breakfast the following day, a written summary of the key points, admonitions and conclusions reached by each of the workshops was presented to each participant in preparations for the second workshop. During this workshop, participants were instructed to develop, as fully as possible, one or more research projects which they felt fit the prescriptions arising from the first workshops and plenary discussions. Following the conference, each of the participants was sent a questionnaire asking him/her to comment further on the issues and methods conceived at the conference and to relate these to his/her own research projects.

We are grateful to the co-organizers of the conference, Julian Cattaneo and Betty-Jane Punnett, and to all those who helped with its admistration especially Pat Lown and Rachana Raizada. Special thanks is due to Hans Schollhammer whose encouragement was critical to the success of the project, to Dean Eric West who supported the conference with critical resources, and to the Social Sciences and Humanities Research Council of Canada for their financial support.

Table of Contents

1 Why Relevance in International Management Research?

Durhane Wong-Rieger
University of Windsor

1.1 Introduction

This book and the conference on which it is based are concerned with the problem of relevance in international management (IM) research. In particular, it seeks to answer the criticism that IM research is not very useful, namely, that is does not deal with important, timely issues; that it lags behind rather than guides practice; that it is North American rather than worldwide in its perspective; that it dwells on the dealings of gigantic multinationals and ignores alternative partnering arrangements (Casson, 1988); and that it has only a limited time perspective, thus providing a static rather than a dynamic understanding of the field.

This chapter sets forth the rationale for achieving relevance in IM research and discusses some of the obstacles to achieving it. It draws, in particular, upon commentaries surrounding organizational development and strategy. The conception of this book was strongly influenced by the papers from two previous conferences addressing similar themes in other areas of organizational science. The first is *Producing Useful Knowledge for Organizations*, edited by Kilmann et al., (1983). The other is *Doing Research that is Useful for Theory and Practice*, edited by Lawler, Mohrman, Mohrman, Ledford, and Cummings (1985).

1.2 Overview of the Problem of Relevance

The conference sought to provide some answers to the criticism that IM research is not very useful. This problem of relevance is not limited to the field of international management. Indeed, business schools have been sharply criticized for their failure to generate practical, useful knowledge in all areas of organizational science (Kilmann, Slevin & Thomas, 1983;

Argyris, 1985), including organizational behavior, organization and management theory, organization development, and finance theory. In all cases, the reasons for the gap between academics and practice are similar. These are evidenced by the lack of concern on the part of (university-based) researchers to make their findings available to managers in a form which is understandable and transformable in actions. Thus, while most academics would ascribe to the view that research must meet the scientific standards for validity, reliability, rigor and precision, they are less likely to be knowledgeable about or concerned with meeting criteria for relevance (Louis, 1983).This is not to suggest that theoretical or methodological issues are less important than practical outcomes. The fact that we are able to raise these criticisms attests to the level to which IM research has begun to satisfy the former concerns. David Ricks (1988) noted in his opening address at the conference that the 1983 issue of the *Journal of International Business Studies* (JIBS) represented a milestone in the field of IM research in that it outlined the requirements for international business research, namely the need for theoretical grounding and methodological rigor. The question here is whether that research also needs to be useful to the practice of international management; in essence, should the standards by which research is judged refer to both theoretical value and practical interest (Walton, 1985)?

In broad terms, the challenges before the IM researcher are similar to those experienced by the manager. In this respect, the good researcher may borrow skills from the good manager (which, incidentally, could enhance communication and mutual understanding, thus increasing the potential for greater usefulness). Borrowing from the field of management, then, three questions are raised in this introductory chapter. First, are IM researchers more concerned with "studying things right" than "studying the right things"? Second, is IM research market-driven? And, third, what does the researcher's own organizational system reward?

In terms of the first question, the situation is somewhat analogous to that of the manager who continues to do the work which should be done by his/her staff. When asked why, the manager is likely to respond, "To make sure it's done right, of course!". As Drucker noted, managers are people who are so busy trying to do things right, they never get around to doing the right things (Drucker, 1974:45–46). The same applies to IM researchers. As scientists and academics sensitized to theoretical and methodological concerns, we are so intent on studying the issue properly that we fail to ask whether it is worth studying or whether there's some other problem which is really more important. Like our managerial counterparts, our strategy, in many cases, is to simplify and reduce the problem to a few variables, to strip it of "confounding noise" variations, and to attempt to fit it to our preconceived hypothetical understandings.

The second question, whether IM research is market driven, might be phrased as, "Who is the consumer?". Is research directed towards the practitioner or is there, as Argyris (1985) suggests, a "user gap", so that most managers will be unaware of research or, if aware, unable to effect the transfer to their own situations? Driver (1979) in reference to human resources models, complained that these were often so ingenious, rigorous, or mathematically complex that they are unusable even by the Human Resources (HR) professional, let alone the practicing manager. Moreover, the academic journals and periodicals which serve as the primary outlets for IM research, make it unlikely that most practitioners would have access to the academic findings. In this same vein, we would also criticize the other major avenue for dissemination of research findings, the academic conference, where practitioners are conspicuously absent. As noted by Pursell at the 1988 AIB Conference (Pursell, 1988), such conferences are not meaningful to either the executive or the consultant and appear, for the most part, as "academics talking to academics". The consumer is clearly not the practitioner.

Common wisdom notwithstanding, building a better mouse-trap does not guarantee that the world will beat a path to your doorstep (Birnberg et al., 1983) if it is not properly packaged and delivered and, preferably, accompanied by explicit instructions on how to set it up and where to put it. Research with potential relevance does not necessarily get translated into practice unless would-be users are made aware of it or are shown how it can be used. Moreover, it is apparent that the attachment of an addendum, which suggests how the research might be applied, is insufficient to overcome the aforementioned objections: rather, there is a need to draw out the linkages and help make the insights transferable to real-world problems as they are experienced.

The third question addresses the institutional barriers to more relevant research. Thomas and Kilmann (1983) reported on a survey which they conducted with approximately 1,000 members of the Academy of Management. According to the responses received from the academics in the sample, there was a considerable discrepancy between their feeling of how much utility research should have and how much it actually had. While the majority reported that they valued equally relevance (defined as "usefulness of a study for practitioner decisions and actions") and rigor (defined as "methodological and logical properties of the study which give confidence in findings"), they also felt that the system in the institutions rewarded rigor over relevance. Moreover, a substantial percentage also felt that their colleagues considered relevance to be of minor or no importance and that the primary purpose of the research appearing in academic journals was knowledge of organizational phenomena for its own sake and not for practice.

1.3 Why Academic Research Cannot Change

The reasons why academic research appears unable to change are quite complex. Perhaps the first question which needs to be asked is why IM researchers don't feel compelled to make their research more useful to practitioners. One answer is because researchers and practitioners inhabit very separate worlds. Managers don't get involved in academic research for practical reasons . The work schedules of senior-level managers seldom allow this and there is little payoff, financial or otherwise. Executives and managers are rarely allocated release time for research activities which are not directly applicable to improvements in the bottom line. Those who "give" of their time to researchers do so at the peril missing their own deadlines.and coming under fire from their superiors.

Why, however, don't researchers get involved with the practical problems of the organizations they are studying? The reasons are manifold. The first is similar to the manager's dilemma; there are few academic rewards for engaging in practical research. It is not only more time-consuming (to foster corporate cooperation, build alliances, and manage relationships) but there are fewer outlets for problem-centered research. Practitioner journals are not revered by the academic world. A second reason is that IM researchers are more comfortable with the academic approach. Most come from traditional disciplines and are well schooled in traditional research methodology. Third, and equally importantly, many do not possess management skills such as communications, problem solving, conflict management, team building, organizational design, and organizational change which are the essential tools of the manager and, by extrapolation, necessary for the academic who wishes to engage in organizational problem-solving.

Why, then, don't academics have more applied skills? Quite simply, unless they have acquired them elsewhere, graduates from business schools (and related Ph. D. programs, such as organizational/industrial psychology), do not receive training in basic managerial competencies. As suggested previously, business schools, for the most part, do not see their primary role as that of management development (Lupton, 1983).

Why don't the institutions emphasize managerial skills in addition to research skills? Part of the answer seemingly stems from the philosophy and values of established faculty members who have themselves been trained in the scientific model. Lawler noted (1985:15) that despite the conviction that changes in graduate training are needed, there was a tendency on the part of faculty to try to replicate what they had gone through as the initiation rite that everybody else had to go through. In addition, senior faculty members play a major role in defining the types of research done by the junior faculty members, either by providing them with collaborative opportunities or by determining the values by which research will be evaluated and rewarded.

The parallel to the organizational situation is clear. Successful researchers, like managers, tend to follow the path which is valued and rewarded. Why, then, do academic institutions value the traditional model of research? Why does research with practical outcomes carry a connotation of being less legitimate than research "purely" for the sake of science?

Quite clearly, in order for academic researchers to move towards a more pragmatic orientation, there need to be corresponding changes in the academic institutions. Changes which would legitimize the latter type of research would need to occur in the professional values systems and outlets for research as well as in the financial and promotional systems of the universities (Goodman, 1985). An ideal model is for the institutions to develop separate applied research unit, such as the Institute for Social Research at the University of Michigan or the Center for Effective Organizations at the University of Southern California. In most cases, the legitimacy of practice-oriented studies will be determined by the ability of the institutions to develop an alternative set of values and standards. Whetten suggests that those who pursue careers with both theoretical and practical relevance will need to be judged with a different set of criteria, perhaps on the basis of a broader range of professional contributions, including activities outside of the academy. Moreover, journals will need to ask authors to place greater emphasis on the implications of their research and to evaluate submission for both utility and validity.

1.4 References

Argyris, C. (1985). Making Knowledge More Relevant to Practice: Maps for Action. In E.E. Lawler III, A.M. Mohrman Jr., A.A. Mohrman, G.E. Ledford, Jr., and T.G. Cummings (eds.), *Doing Research that is Useful for Theory and Practice.* San Francisco: Jossey-Bass, 79–106.

Birnberg, J.G., L. Turopolec and S.M. Young (1983). The Marketing of Academic Research: An Example from Accounting. In R.H. Kilmann, K.W. Thomas, D.P. Slevin, R. Nath and S.L. Jerrell (eds.), *Producing Useful Knowledge for Organizations.* New York: Praeger, 634–655.

Casson, M. (1988). Recent Trends in International Business: A New Analysis. Paper presented to Inaugural Research Conference of the Ontario Center for International Business, Toronto.

Driver, M.J. (1979). Individual Decision Making and Creativity. In S. Kerr (ed.). Organizational behavior. Columbus, Ohio: Grid Press, 78–92.

Drucker, P. F. (1974). *Management: Tasks, Responsibilities, Practices.* Harper and Row: New York.

Goodman, P.S. (1985). Critical Issues in Doing Research that Contributes to Theory and Practice. In E.E. Lawler III, A.M. Mohrman Jr., A.A. Mohrman, G.E. Ledford, Jr., and T.G. Cummings (eds.). *Doing Research that is Useful for Theory and Practice.* San Francisco: Jossey-Bass, 324–342.

Kilmann, R.H., K.W. Thomas, D.P. Slevin, R. Nath and S.L. Jerrell (eds.). (1983). *Producing Useful Knowledge for Organizations.* New York: Praeger.

Lawler III, E.E. (1985). Challenging Traditional Research Assumptions. In E.E. Lawler III, A.M. Mohrman Jr., A.A. Mohrman, G.E. Ledford, Jr., and T.G. Cummings (eds.). *Doing Research that is Useful for Theory and Practice.* San Francisco: Jossey-Bass, 1–17.

Louis, M.R. (1983). Useful knowledge and the Knowledge User: Toward Explicit Meanings. In R.H. Kilmann, K.W. Thomas, D.P. Slevin, R. Nath and S.L. Jerrell (eds.), *Producing Useful Knowledge for Organizations.* New York: Praeger, 25–36.

Lupton, T. (1983). Functions and Organization of University Business Schools. In R.H. Kilmann, K.W. Thomas, D.P. Slevin, R. Nath and S.L. Jerrell (eds.). *Producing Useful Knowledge for Organizations.* New York: Praeger, 582–599.

Pursell, W. (1988). Relevant Research for International Managers: A

Practitioners View. Paper presented at Annual Conference of the Academy of International Business. San Diego, California, November.

Ricks, D. (1988). Research Topics in International Management. Paper presented at Conference on Research for Relevance in International Management. University of Windsor, Ontario, June.

Thomas, K. W. and Kilmann, R. H. (1983). Where Have the Organizational Sciences Gone? A Survey of the Academy of Management Membership. In R.H. Kilmann, K.W. Thomas, D.P. Slevin, R. Nath and S.L. Jerrell (eds.). *Producing Useful Knowledge for Organizations.* New York: Praeger, 69–81.

Walton, R. E. (1985). Strategies with Dual Relevance. In E.E. Lawler III, A.M. Mohrman Jr., A.A. Mohrman, G.E. Ledford, Jr., and T.G. Cummings (eds.), *Doing Research that is Useful for Theory and Practice.* San Francisco: Jossey-Bass, 79–106.

2 International Management Research: Past, Present, and Future

David Ricks
Thunderbird Graduate School

2.1 Progress in International Management Research to Date

We can be proud of how much we have learned about the management of multinational enterprises, especially since the field of international management is so young. In fact, most of the earliest research pioneers are still with us today.

The Fall 1983 Special Issue of *The Journal of International Business Studies* (JIBS) by Professors Dymsza, Negandhi, and Adler, contains some especially enlightening research. In some ways that issue, in which problems of data collection and data analysis were addressed, may mark a turning point in the field. Up until then it was not uncommon to see articles in which researchers simply compared a certain management practice in two countries. As we read more and more of these reports we became exposed to large quantities of data, but found it difficult to use. Furthermore, many of the studies lacked a sufficient theoretical grounding.

Simple comparative studies now seem to be falling out of favor, especially those studies which are not sufficiently grounded in other literature or make no attempt to develop theory. Current thinking seems to be that theory must be considered. For example, many of today's JIBS reviews are now expecting a theoretical dimension in submitted papers. Papers which neglect this dimension are often judged as failing to make enough of a contribution to warrant publication.

It has been nine years since that special 1983 issue of JIBS was published and yet many suggestions made by the authors have been overlooked. Perhaps it is now time to pull that issue off our shelves and re-examine it, especially the articles by Anant Negandhi, Nancy Adler, George England and Itzhak Harpaz, Uma Sekaran, and Geert Hofstede. These articles address important problems of data collection as well as data analysis. Manuscripts submitted to JIBS usually contain problems in at least one of these two areas, problems which could have been avoided had the authors followed the suggestions and recommendations in those 1983 articles. Data analysis problems are discouraging, but at least they can usually be solved or corrected. Data collection problems, however, are often fatal for the research project.

2.2 Future Research Topics

That 1983 JIBS issue also contains suggestions for future research topics. Since a great deal of research has been published since then, I felt that an update was appropriate. Rather than simply reporting my opinions, the 1987 program committee members for the International Management Division of the Academy of Management were surveyed for their ideas and opinions. (Committee members are listed in Appendix A.) They were asked to identify the most important research topics in the field of international management for the next five years.

All but three of the committee members responded. Douglas Nigh and I have analyzed the responses (a detailed list of these responses is available upon request), and several patterns have emerged.

The first thing that became apparent was that there is no shortage of ideas. Literally hundreds of different research topics were suggested. In fact, the rather surprising thing was that very few were repeated.

Many of the suggested research topics can be grouped into the following traditional categories:

1. Strategic Management
2. Human Resource Management
3. Organizational Behavior and Cross-national Management
4. Organization and Control
5. Production and Sourcing

However almost one-half of the respondents cited research topics which do not fit as easily into the traditional structure. Most of these research ideas fall into the following categories:

1. Forms of International Involvement
2. Management of Innovation, Information, and Technology
3. Business – Government Relations

The academicians were unable to resist adding suggestions about how we can improve our research methodology. Their ideas can be grouped into the following five areas of concern:

1. the need to develop cross-national research teams;
2. the need for more longitudinal studies;
3. the need for research which is less U. S. oriented;
4. the need for multi-level studies rather than research which is only aimed at the firm level or the national level;
5. the value of quantitative and qualitative research. (A few respondents suggested that perhaps we should use both qualitative and quantitative methods in our research projects.)

In summary, we need to gain a better theoretical and practical understanding of how to effectively manage in an international environment. We have little trouble generating important topics for research and not much trouble analyzing the data we obtain, but we are still having a great deal of difficulty collecting the appropriate data correctly. We've made progress in all areas of research, but we still have a long way to go.

2.3 Appendix

Table 2.1 *IMD Program Committee 1987*

Nance J. Adler	Briance Mascarenhas
B. Ram Baliga	Edwin L. Miller
Bhal J. Bhatt	Richard Moxon
Jean J. Boddewyn	Anan Phatak
Joseph Cheng	Douglas Nigh
William H. Davidson	Richard B. Peterson
William G. Egelhoff	Arvind Phatik
John Garland	Thomas A. Poynter
Thomas N. Gladwin	S. Benjamin Prasad
Robert E. Grosse	Franklin R. Root
Stephen E. Guisinger	Kendal Roth
Michael J. Jedel	Hans Schollhammer
Lane Kelley	S. Prakash Sethi
Ken I. Kim	Jeremiah J. Sullivan
Stephen J. Korbin	Brian Toyne
Bruce Kogut	Yoshi Tsurumi
Duane Kujawa	Rosalie L. Tung
Donald J. Lecraw	
Davis A. Ricks – Program Chair	

3 Future Directions in International Comparative Management Research

Richard B. Peterson
University of Washington

3.1 Introduction

As a past Chair of the International Management Division, I think it is important that we assess the state of our field. I sense that the next few years represent a very crucial period in the history of international management research. The profession has grown considerably in recent years. The Board of Governors of the Academy has been looking at the issue of internationalizing the organization. Yet if one looks at the major journals and the yearly program of the Academy, one is struck by how insular most on our research is. There is an underlying assumption that our findings for American samples have wide applicability to how organizations (and people) operate in other nations. While human beings share a basic commonality of needs, there is no assurance they manifest them in the same ways.

International management researchers can contribute to decreasing the insularity of the Academy and nurturing its internationalization. However, in order to do so we must put our own house in order. Now is the time to examine the strengths and weaknesses of our research. More importantly, we need to look ahead in providing an agenda for future research in International and Comparative Management. If we do not, it is likely that we will continue to do research in the way it has been done in the past. We will also miss out on opportunities to both define our field within the academic community as well as to provide help to the international practitioner community.

This paper begins by briefly summarizing where we have come from in postwar research in International and Comparative Management. We highlight some of the major reviews of cross-cultural management research as well as explanatory models. The second section provides a short summary of the shortcomings of our research as they have been noted by various critics over the years. Finally, the major part of this paper outlines an agenda for International and Comparative Management research in the coming years.

3.1.1 Origin and Progression

We are indebted to anthropologists for most of our present understanding of "culture". Anthropologists have a rich tradition in studying non-industrial societies through use of ethnographic methods. Levi-Strauss, Malinowski, Benedict, White, Geertz, and others have provided us with a wealth of key concepts and models for understanding the role of culture. However, few anthropologists have concentrated on understanding the behavior of employees and managers in industrial societies.

Comparative management research is largely a post-World War II phenomenon. This is especially true for American scholars who journeyed to various parts of the world as part of projects encouraging economic development. Many of the earliest studies were done by economists such as Harbison and Meyers (1959) and Granick (1962). They were largely descriptive studies based on readings and on-site interview with executives, managers, union leaders, and government officials. While these academics recognized diversity in managerial behavior across nations, many of them were committed to the notion that the industrializing imperative would lead to convergence by the industrial nations over time. A number of these early studies benefited from funding by the Ford Foundation.

In the 1960's management researchers became quite interested in international and comparative management issues. The best known study at that time was done by Haire, Ghiselli, and Porter (1966) based on questionnaire data from managers in 14 countries. They concluded that managerial behavioral had elements of both universalism and particularism. Some 28 % of the cross-national differences were accounted for by cultural explanations. Their findings gave support both to the universalists (convergence theorists) and cultural relativists. Surprisingly, this this did not deter many management scholars from accepting the position that management behavior was universal.

The message of Servan-Schrieber in *The American Challenge* (1968) provided strong support for the position that America was at the leading edge. Countries hoping to compete with the United States would have to accommodate American ways of managing and American technology.

McClelland (1961) and his colleagues said essentially the same thing. They stressed the importance of need for achievement and entrepreneurial outlook in a society if that nation was to have significant economic growth.

Social science research methodology spread to American business schools in the late 1960's and early 1970's. Descriptive studies, no matter how well done, became passé. In recent years there has been a considerable amount of research published in our area. While some of it is still descriptive, the vast majority of studies are empirical tests of international or comparative management using correlations, regression, and multivariate statistics.

Where are we in terms of the development of our field? A number of major books and articles have been written over the past twenty-five years to help us assess the nature of the "beast" called International and Comparative Management. We shall discuss a representative set of these reviews and critiques.

Farmer and Richman, in their book *Comparative Management and Economic Progress* (1965) presented a way of modeling the field of comparative management. Unfortunately, few researchers ever used all or part of the model as a foundation for their own research. Undoubtedly, most researchers were overwhelmed by the sheer number of variables and subvariables identified. The 1960's represented a time when most of us in the field thought we would provide answers to the "big picture" by looking simultaneously at economic, social, political, and cultural factors that helped us to understand and explain cross-national management behavior. We later drew back from such grand expectations.

In 1970 Boddewyn and Ajiferuke provided an important review and critique of comparative management. They found that studies could be categorized into three major groupings: economic, psychological, and sociological. The disciplinary inclination of the researcher largely explained the variables chosen as well as the interpretation of the study findings.

In the same year Roberts (1970) presented a very pessimistic view of cross-cultural organizational research based on her review of the literature. Fortunately, many of us continued to believe that research in comparative management was worthwhile. Many of us were even willing to accept the fact that our research might not always meet the rigors of an experimental psychologist or econometrician. Schollhammer (1973) and others wrote periodic reviews and critiques of our field during the 1970's, but in general, there was not much examination of the state of the field.

The past few years have evidenced a real surge of interest in international management. This can be seen in the rapid growth in The International Management Division of the Academy of Management (IMD), comparative management conferences, concern for internationalizing the management curriculum, and the writings and research on comparative management. Illustrative critical works include Bhagat and Mcquaid (1982), Adler (1983, 1986) and Ronen (1986). What have we learned in terms of our research in International and Comparative Management? The next section very briefly summarizes the shortcomings of much of our research.

3.1.2 Shortcomings of our Research

One might ask why we examine our shortcomings. After all, other members of our profession pointed them out to us in various critiques of cross-cultural research over the years. Unfortunately, however, this has not deterred us from continuing to make some of the same mistakes. Ideally, we would have such a list before us every time we sat down to design another comparative management study. If we did so, the field of cross-cultural management research would advance more quickly.

Many of the following points have been made elsewhere, but they need to be repeated so that we can move forward. The shortcomings include:

3.1.2.1 Lack of Theoretical Base

All too many of our studies have neglected to test theoretical or conceptual models to put our results in a broader framework. The work of Marsh and Mannari (1976) on testing Goldthorpe's instrumental theory of the worker with Japanese employees' behavior is one of the notable exceptions.

3.1.2.2 Ethnocentrism

While particularly noticeable in the 1950's and 1960's, we still tend to adhere to the assumption that companies in other nations should be compared to the Western industrial model. Dore's (1973) study of a British and Japanese factory provides an exception by noting the possibility that Japan may be the best model for late industrializing nations.

3.1.2.3 Heavy Reliance on Convenience Samples

While understandable, such samples rarely allow real comparability in doing research across countries. A sample of textile workers in Jakarta, Indonesia may not be the best for comparison with Houston, Texas oil workers or Japanese electronics employees in Osaka. Cole's (1979) study of automotive workers in Detroit and Yokohama is a good illustration of what we should be using as samples.

3.1.2.4 Over-emphasis on Cultural Variance

It is important that we not lose sight of the similarities across nations. Too often we simply emphasize how Chinese are different from French and so on. We also need to look at variances within a culture (nation) rather than assuming that all Americans, for example, share a common cultural way of viewing the world. The earlier work of Kluckhohn and Strodtbeck (1962) reminds us of the dangers of not recognizing within-cultural differences.

3.1.2.5 Study Limited to One Nation

Many of our studies have not really been comparative at all. Rather, they have looked at the situation in one non-U. S. country without being able to relate their findings to those of other nations. Graves' (1973) study of Japanese and American workers offer models of what we should be doing.

3.1.2.6 Problems of Linguistic Meanings

Whether the questionnaire is translated or not, most cross-cultural studies fail to take into account the limitations of language in conveying equivalent meaning in two or more languages. Haire, Ghiselli, and Porter (1966) were wise to point this out in their interpretation of findings showing that the Japanese shared similar democratic values with the Americans and the British.

3.1.2.7 Assuming that Important Factors in One Nation Have Equal Value in Another Nation

American researchers in the early postwar years assumed that all employees shared a common desire for participation. Whyte (1969) pointed out the fallacy of this position in his study of Peruvian railroad workers.

3.1.2.8 Reliance on a Single Research Method

The vast majority of the cross-cultural management studies have relied heavily on one method of gaining information; namely, questionnaires. This has not allowed us to delve more deeply into the meaning of our data though supplementary methods such as interviews, participant-observation, behavioral scenarios, and so forth. Our (Peterson and Schwind, 1977) work on personnel problems in multinational companies included interviews of expatriates and interviews with both middle management and executive officials.

3.1.2.9 Limitations of Cross-cultural Studies

Such studies provide us with an image of reality that is confined to one point in time. The test of convergence vs. cultural relativism can only be answered by providing shots of reality in international studies over time. There is a real paucity of solidly grounded longitudinal research that could help us to answer whether organizational behavior over time is becoming more similar or not. Whitehill and Takezawa's follow-up study (1968) of Japanese and American workers is one illustration of what needs to be done. However, even that study needs periodic updating.

3.1.2.10 Lack of Data to Support Conclusions

Many studies of the Japanese employment system fall in this category. The assumption is that the Japanese lifetime employment system and its pillars have not changed in large firms. Yet some descriptive (Rohlen, 1979) and anecdotal articles suggest that there are important modifications in how the system really operates in light of the two major oil crises. We need company-supplied records to see how promotions and pay increases really take place over time. Do they strictly adhere to the *nenko* system of promotion and compensation?

3.1.2.11 Bias Towards Studying Large Companies

The vast majority of companies studied have been quite large. This does not tell us much about smaller firms. Cole's (1971) study of working life in smaller Japanese factories is a model for research that would allow us to distinguish organizational behavior in smaller firms.

3.1.2.12 Rare Instances of Using Samples of Employees and Managers Across Hierarchical Levels Across Nations

The more common situation is to drawn a sample of production, clerical-administrative, or managerial employees and then draw broad conclusions about organizational behavior from their answers to attitudinal and behavior questions. Thus we are unable to fully test whether the answers are cultural-specific or partially affected by the type of work they do or their position in the hierarchy.

3.1.2.13 Failure to State and Test *a priori* Hypotheses

Many of the earliest studies collected data and than reported results without identifying what they expected to find in light of the literature. More recent studies have paid closer attention to the need to move beyond the exploratory stage to state expected results based on solid foundations in the research literature.

3.1.2.14 Over-emphasis on Studying Attitudes Rather than Behaviors

Our field continues to be beset by too much reliance on attitudinal perceptions. It is well to know how people feel about their jobs, the company and so forth. However, specific attitudes can be nothing more than options. We really need to shift more of our energies to testing for how people really behave. Questionnaires prove less helpful in this domain while scenarios and participation-observation represent more fruitful ways of gaining access to such behavioral data.

3.1.2.15 Imbalance in Terms of Areas of the World Studied

A review of the comparative management research literature shows that many studies have been done in a small number of Western European countries and Japan. We still know very little about the Mediterranean countries, Eastern Bloc countries, the Middle East, Africa, and Latin America. Asia is an emerging giant and yet we are virtually "babes in the woods" in understanding both the diversity and commonality of organizational behavior there.

3.1.2.16 Failure to Articulate Cultural and Other Explanations

In all too many cases the researchers have not articulated the reasons why we should expect, for instance, that Malaysian agricultural employees would expect a different way of interacting with their bosses than would be true of their counterparts in France. One has the feeling that some of the researchers have not delved into the germane literature that would serve as a framework for stating hypotheses. For my own part, the real excitement in International and Comparative Management is in hearing about what makes people in one culture or nation different from people in other cultures. That is why books by Christopher (1983) are so exciting to read since he has lived in Japan and has a close acquaintance with its people.

Keeping these past research weaknesses in mind, we need to look at where International and Comparative Management research should go in the coming years. The views expressed in the final section of this paper are mine. Hopefully, they will serve as a basis for discourse within the community of international management researchers.

3.2 A Future Agenda

There are several main points that will be discussed in this final section. They include: (1) what issues we study; (2) how we study the issue; and (3) some illustrative cases for research in the coming years.

3.2.1 What We Study

We need to begin by addressing the most important question first; namely, what is the significance of the topic, issue, or problem that we wish to investigate? A review of the past research suggests that many studies, however well intentioned, were limited in their applicability. A comparative study of leadership in five nations does not really tell us anything more than leadership styles may vary across nations in terms of business leaders' responses. There is no explanatory link to how certain leadership styles are associated with meaningful outcomes such as corporate performance. Are the links only in one direction or does profitability itself lead to change in desirable leadership styles?

It is important that we as researchers keep in mind the objective of separating "the forest from the trees". We need to see the broad picture rather than be immersed in the details. One helpful procedure is to ask ourselves how we might justify our study to our fellow researchers, our granting agencies, or the executives of firms we wish to study. How do our results help to develop or elucidate theory, improve management practice, and/or change organizational policies? What can people learn from our research?

It seems to me that an increasing part of organizational behavior research is moving towards the reductionist end of the continuum. I fear that international management researchers could be caught in the same trap of trying to emulate the latest methodological techniques of the experimental psychologists. There is strong support for these values by many people serving on the editorial boards of most of our major management journals. I would hope that we can be more catholic in recognizing the diversity of research design approaches. While drawing on the methodologies of the experimental psychologists, we need to encourage solidly grounded descriptive research, new theory building and testing, philosophical essays, and model building based on what we already know.

Most of us now recognize that culture, by itself, cannot explain the vast majority of differences in the economic success of various nations. However, by testing cultural theories alongside convergence theory and other explanatory models, we can gain a sense of its relative contribution. We need to design our studies so as to capture the complexity of organizational life. In so doing, we will be taking an important step in making our field of International and Comparative Management relevant to decision-makers, by asking, and seeking answers, to significant questions.

3.2.2 How We Study the Issue

Once we have answered the question of significance, we need to ask ourselves how we might best go about studying the issue. I much prefer reading some of the older literature by people like Granick (1962) and Hartmann (1959) than many micro-behavioral studies using sophisticated statistical techniques. Those colleagues spent sufficient time to capture the essential elements of what they were studying. Long questionnaires, no matter how carefully crafted often miss the real essence of what we are studying. Data analysis is a poor second choice to in-depth reading and personal interviews with people in other nations.

What steps might we take? We should start by letting the questions we wish to ask be the guide for determining how we do the research. Some of our own doctoral students raise questions about the narrowness of questions asked, issues addressed, and research methods used. We need to listen to their message. In what way have we fallen into the trap of using certain research approaches because of the school we attended. the professor we had, and/or the editorial values of the leading journals?

I am not proposing that we necessarily turn away from laboratory experiments, quasi-experimental field studies, and other designs that use a heavy dosage of statistical tests. Rather, we need to choose the best research design and methodology in light of the content issue or question, not the other way around.

Finally, we should seriously encourage more team research in International and Comparative Management. The vast majority of our studies are single or dual authored. Often the similar training of the authors constrains our ability to address multi-disciplinary questions. We still suffer from the tendency to explain the elephant only in terms of our own values and education. Thus the psychologists, sociologists, political scientists and economists all have their own interpretation of truth. Individually, they all fall short of grasping the diverse elements of the issue, question, or problem.

These are reasons for encouraging team research other than cross-disciplinary advantages. Cost is an important factor. At one time the vast majority of our research was done by American academics travelling abroad, many with grants or on sabbatical leave. More often than not, local academicians were used primarily for contact purposes rather than as research colleagues. In the late 1960's the foundations largely withdrew from funding our research unless it could show a strong policy impact. Business firms did not pick up the slack. The result was that large scale studies like the Inter-University Project funded by Ford Foundation could no longer be done.

Team research using people from several countries reduces the cost of travel and field research so that a study of management in two countries can involve the native team member collecting much of the data in his or her own country.

Team research has a further benefit. It allows for the researchers themselves to participate in acculturation by the give-and-take discussion among the cross-national team members. I have traveled and lived abroad on many occasions, and yet, I realize how many cultural biases I have had in trying to interpret employee and managerial behavior in other countries. The physical and natural scientists have used team research for decades with considerable success. We could gain from their experience.

3.3 Illustrative Cases

There are a multiplicity of questions, issues and problems in International and Comparative Management that we might address in the coming years. We shall only discuss a few of them here as examples of what I hope we will be doing in the remaining years of this century. The choice is biased by my own research on cross-cultural management. Others of you will be able to suggest a variety of other topics.

First, can we really generalize from our cross-national management samples to the values, beliefs, and attitudes of the broader society? To what extent are studies done by INSEAD faculty (Laurent, 1983) on managers from the United States and various European countries valid for all adult members of the respective nation? Are there ways that French managers are partially un-French in their value orientation? What makes the structure offirms distinct from the organizational design used in the British Department of the Environment? What makes them similar? Are executives in large Japanese corporations change-makers or are they primarily upholders of continuity in Japanese society? These are important questions we should be addressing.

Second, what impact does culture really play in national economic performance? Does being raised in the United States, Japan, or West Germany help us to explain why these nations have stood out as economic giants in the postwar period? Is the discipline of the West German worker, the ambition of the American manager, or the "fitting in" of Japanese employees paramount in explaining international economic performance? What then are the lessons for developing nations from our research? Should they seek to emulate us to develop their own culturally-dominant values and priorities? Or is it really the quality of the educational system or access to raw materials that differentiates national performance?

Third, which factors really explain variance in organizational performance, job satisfaction, strategy and organizational structure? Cross-disciplinary teams of researchers could design studies that seek to "tease out" the impact of cultural, political, social, and economic theories on corporate and employee performance. We have never really definitively tested the efficacy of these multiple explanatory theories.

Finally, what can we say about the long term? For example, is the Japanese employment system changing in response to the oil shocks and increasing competition for world markets from the newly industrializing countries like Taiwan, South Korea, and Singapore? The data is quite scanty. We need to track the Japanese employment system in large firms over time to know what is happening. Is it continuity or change or even both? There a crying need for well designed longitudinal research to answer such questions. These kinds of studies will require solid funding.

In closing, I hope that this paper has provided you with some "food for thought". I trust that my remarks will encourage a dialog within the profession in the coming years.

3.4 References

Adler, N.J. (1983). A Typology of Management Studies Involving Culture. *Journal of International Business Studies,* 14, 2, 29–47.

Adler, N.J. (1986). *International Dimensions of Organizational Behavior.* Boston: Kent Publishing Company.

Bhagat, R. and S.J. McQuaid (1982). Role of Subjective Culture in Organizations: Review and Directions for Future Research. *Journal of Applied Psychology,* October, 653–685.

Boddewyn, J. and M. Ajiferuke (1970). Culture and Other Explanatory Variables in Comparative Management Studies. *Academy of Management Journal,* June, 153–163.

Christopher, R.C. (1983). *The Japanese Mind: The Goliath Explained.* New York: The Linden Press/Simon and Schuster.

Cole, R. (1971). *Japanese Blue Collar: The Changing Tradition.* Berkeley and Los Angeles: University of California.

Cole, R. (1979). *Work, Mobility, and Participation: A Comparative Study of American and Japanese Industry.* Berkeley and Los Angeles: University of California Press.

Dore, R. (1973). *British Factory-Japanese Factory.* Berkeley and Los Angeles: University of California Press.

Farmer, R. and B. Richman (1965). *Comparative Management and Economic Progress.* Homewood, IL: Richard D. Irwin.

Granick, D. (1962). *The European Executive.* New York: Doubleday.

Graves, D. (1973). *Management Research-A Cross-Cultural Perspective.* London: Elsevier Scientific Publishing Company.

Haire, M., E. Ghiselli and L. Porter (1966). *Managerial Thinking*. New York: John Wiley.

Harbison, F. and Meyers C.A. (1959). *Management in the Industrial World: An International Analysis*. New York: McGraw Hill.

Hartmann, H. (1959). *Authority and Organization in German Management*. Princeton: Princeton University Press.

Kluckhohn, C. and F.L. Strodtbeck (1962). *Variations in Value Orientations*. Evanston, IN: Row, Peterson.

Laurent, A. (1983). The Cultural Diversity of Management, Conceptions, *International Studies of Management and Organization,* Spring, 75–96.

Marsh, R. and H. Mannari (1976). *Modernization and the Japanese Factory*. Princeton: Princeton University Press, 1976.

McClelland, D C. (1961). *The Achieving Society*. Princeton: D. Van Nostrand.

Nakane, C. (1970). *Japanese Society*. Berkeley and Los Angeles: University of California Press.

Peterson, R. B. and H. Schwind (1977). A Comparative Study of Personnel Problems in International Companies and Joint Ventures in Japan. *Journal of International Business Studies,* Spring-Summer, 45–55.

Roberts, K. H. (1970). On Looking at an Elephant: An Evaluation of Cross-Cultural Research Related to Organizations. *Psychology Bulletin,* November, 327–350.

Rohlen, T. (1979). Permanent Employment Faces Recession, Slow Growth and Aging Work Force, *Journal of Japanese Studies,* Summer, 235–272.

Ronen, S. (1986). *Comparative and Multinational Management*. New York: John Wiley and Sons.

Schollhammer, H.(1973). Strategies and Methodologies in International Business and Comparative Management Research, *Management and International Review,* 6, 16–27.

Servan-Schrieber, J-J. (1968). *The American Challenge*. New York: Antheneum.

Triandis, H. (1972). *The Analysis of Subjective Culture*. New York: Wiley Intersciences.

Whitehill, A. M. and S. Takezawa (1968). *The Other Worker*. Honolulu: East-West Center Press.

Whyte, W. F. (1969). Culture and Work. In R.A. Webber (ed.) *Culture and Management*. Homewood, IL: Irwin. 30–39.

4 Global Firms and Nation-States

Stephen J. Kobrin
Wharton School, University of Pennsylvania

4.1 Global Firms and Global Competition

Some early observers of the multinational corporation argued that the emerging reorganization of the world economy rendered nation-states, and state borders, atavistic barriers to a more efficient global division of labor. George Ball (1968:164) for example, labeled nation-states, "archaic concepts unsympathetic to the needs of our complex world" and called for transnational integration though denationalized MNC's.

Although the state has not withered in the face of the MNC's either in practice or the literature, large, integrated, transnational firms have made a difference in the structure of relations between, and the distribution of power among states. In this paper I first briefly attempt to define what I mean by the global firm and global competition, then briefly outline the development and structure of the existing state system, and last try to assess the likely impact of the former upon the latter.

A number of authors have noted that concepts such as the global firm and global competition are not clearly defined[1]. Stephen Hymer (1976) formulated his theory of foreign direct investment by seeking the advantage possessed by the MNC that allows it to offset the disadvantages of cultural and geographic distance and compete with a local firm. A variant of that question can be used to order the concept of global competition: what are the competitive advantages (vis-à-vis a domestic firm) resulting from international investment and operations? As Bruce Kogut observes,

---

[1] For example, Gary Hammel and C.K. Prahalad (1985).

the question is then, "how international activity augments or creates strategic advantages" (Kogut, 1984:152). I suggest a threefold typology[2]:

4.1.1 Exploitation of Differences in Factor Prices/Resource Allocation

International firms gain competitive advantage from access to more abundant/cheaper factors of production abroad: they exploit differences in national comparative advantage. For example, a firm can produce components where labor is relatively cheap and productive, locate energy intensive refining operations where hydroelectric power is abundant, or locate technology-intensive operations in countries with high levels of education.[3]

4.1.2 Multinational Operations

Integrated, centrally controlled multinational operations provide sources of competitive advantage such as the ability to transfer learning across markets, increased returns to basic research and development, exploitation of ambiguous national jurisdiction, subsidization across markets, diversification of economic or political risks, and the ability to scan for new technologies or market opportunities worldwide. Although it is rarely articulated precisely in the literature, the concept of global competition assumes that firms gain operational advantages from a presence in all, or most, significant markets worldwide.

4.1.3 Transnational Economies of Scale

In a number of critical industries many (if not most) national markets are too small to support efficient business activity. In some, plant level economies of scale cannot be achieved with volume generated by a reasona-

---

[2] The typology is not original and reflects arguments in Kogut (1984). It is similar to that of Porter (exploiting differences in markets across countries, economies of scale, or economies of scope) which is reflected in Goshal (1987). See Porter (1985) and Goshal (1987).
[3] See Bruce Kogut (1985).

ble market share in a single country (automobiles are an example). In others, (e.g., mainframe computers) most firms' sales in a single market are insufficient to generate the absolute level of research and development expenditures needed to remain competitive. In both situations, firms must integrate transnationally to compete: they must sell relatively standardized products in a number of markets to generate the volume necessary for efficient production of competitive R&D expenditures. In these cases, transnationally integrated firms gain an advantage over domestic competitors. It is important to note that the critical point is reached when domestic firms can no longer compete; when the competitive advantages of international operations are such that a uninational firm is forced from the industry.

4.2 Nation-States and the State System

The modern state is defined in terms of political control over geographic territory and an absence of supranational or central authority. State sovereignty entails ultimate law making and law enforcing authority within a specific geographic area and that requires borders that are both sharply defined and impermeable. Sovereignty over territory, the very essence of the modern state, assumes an ability to provide for the physical security of inhabitants through the maintenance and defense of discrete borders.

In the twentieth century the concept of sovereignty has been extended to include economic as well as political-military security. The modern state is held responsible for macro-economic performance: growth, inflation, external balance, and employment. In most states the regime is also held responsible for some minimal level of welfare and, perhaps, for development and industrialization. Thus, sovereignty as control over territory implies control over the economy and economic actors as well as the polity and military security.

The system of states is characterized by the absence of a central authority and by units that are functionally equivalent as sovereign states exerting control over a discrete territory and population. In its starkest terms it is a self help system structured in terms of differences in relative power between units.[4]

---

[4] See Kenneth Waltz (1979).

In summary, two points are important:

1. states are geographically defined in terms of political control over discrete territory, and
2. as states are functionally equivalent, it is relative power that determines the structure of the system.

4.3 The State and Multinational Firms

I will illustrate impacts of global firms on states in terms of the threefold typology suggested above.

4.3.1 Exploitation of Differences in Factor Allocation

MNC's gain competitive advantage from exploitation of national differences in resource allocation. There are two significant potential impacts on the state system: changes in the resources or wealth of a given state and increases in economic interdependence. I will discuss the former under MNC operations. The latter implies that by providing direct intra-firm links between economies MNCs increase the benefits of trade and capital flows, thus increasing the costs of independence or autonomy and binding polities and economies more closely together.

4.3.2 Multinational Operations

Integrated multinational operations affect the structure of the state system by: 1) facilitating shifts in resources or wealth between states; 2) providing direct transnational links, the web of multinational operations, between states; and 3) reducing state control over economic actors. The first two can directly affect relative power and thus the structure of the system: the latter can affect the nature of interstate relations directly. I provide only limited examples of each.

Foreign direct investment facilitates the shift of factors such as capital and technology across borders and thus shift of factors such as capital and technology across borders and thus economic variables such as employment, output, and external balance in specific states. As it is relative rather than absolute gains that matter in the international political system, such shifts can affect the security of any given state and result in the structure of the system (e.g., from a hegemonic to a multipolar system).

Second, the web of MNC operations changes the nature of relations between states by allowing direct access to territory. The best known examples are efforts by home countries to exert control over subsidiaries of their MNC's located abroad to impose trade sanctions extra-territorially. Host countries, however, have been able to utilize the network in reverse to increase their leverage in home country politics: Canada's use of American automobile companies to increase its leverage in the U. S. Congress is but one example.

Last, the existence of integrated MNCs reduced national control over operations in any given country. The point is well developed in the literature and I will deal with its implications below.

4.3.3 Transnational Scale

As noted above, in a number of industries national markets are too small to support efficient business operations. One can generalize and argue that efficient economic operations require markets larger than that of most states; economic geography and political geography are no longer congruent as the minimal territory required for economic efficiency is larger than that of many states. The implication is clear; if efficient production must be organized transnationally then any given state becomes dependent on the multinational system and there is a significant loss in autonomy and/or independence.

4.4 Implications

I would argue that there is a difference in kind between the impacts of the first two sources of international competitive advantage on states and the third. Impacts resulting from shifting comparative advantage and multinational operations can be significant for both individual states and the structure of the system. However, neither inevitably leads to a major transformation. Although the existence of MNC's and global competition can exacerbate interdependence and increase pressures for some sort of explicit ordering of the system (a regime in technical terms) these changes are consistent with the post-Westphalian structure. Furthermore, there is considerable room for bargaining by individual states and for trade-offs between increased efficiency and other national goals.

The changes in political and economic geography discussed above may have radical implications for the state system. If transnational scale economies are a reality, if minimally efficient operations cannot be achieved without cross-border integration, then national borders, the essence of the state system, may lose some meaning. States may face a stark choice of accepting integration into a transnational productive system over which whey exert only partial control or not participating in certain industries; they may face a zero-one choice rather than a marginal trade-off between efficiency and other national goals.

As noted above, although states certainly retain sovereignty over foreign firms, their control over economic actors and their economy may be compromised by MNC's. The exacerbation of interdependence limits a state's freedom to implement policy autonomously and the existence of coordinated multinational operations comprises territorial sovereignty in the sense of control over economic actors and the economy.

The affects of transnational integration (of global industries), however, represent a difference in kind. They render nation-states (and national borders) much less meaningful as economic units. Given the importance of economics in the modern world, this requires at least a consideration of the viability of territorially defined national units. One must ask what sovereignty, as ultimate control over discrete territory, means in a world where efficiency mandates the transnational organization of production.

4.5 References

Ball, G.W. (1968). Cosmocorp: The Importance of Being Stateless. *Atlantic Community Quarterly* VI (Summer), 163–170.

Ghoshal, S. (1987). Global Stategies: An Organizing Framework. *Strategic Management Journal*, 8, 425–440.

Hamel, G. and C.K. Prahalad (1985) Do you Really Have a Global Strategy? *Harvard Business Review*, July-August, 139–148.

Hymer, S.H. (1976). *The International Operations of Firms: A Study of Foreign Direct Investment.* Cambridge, MA: MIT Press.

Kogut, B. (1984). Normative Observations on the Value Added Chain and Strategic Groups. *Journal of International Business Studies,* 15, Fall, 151–167.

Kogut, B. (1985). Designing Global Strategies: Comparative and Competitive Value-Added Chains. *Sloan Management Review,* 26(4), 15–28.

Porter, M. (1985). *Competitive Advantage.* New York: The Free Press.

Waltz, K. (1979). *Theory of International Politics.* Reading, MA: Addison-Wesley Publishing.

5 Research in International Human Resource Management

Rosalie Tung
Simon Fraser University – Canada
Betty Jane Punnett
University of Windsor – Canada

5.1 Introduction

To date, much research in international human resource management (IHRM) has focused on the staffing policies in subsidiary operations of multinational corporations, the selection and training of personnel for overseas assignments, and select aspects of international assignments, such as the use of women in expatriate assignments. While research on these topics has assisted our understanding of certain aspects of IHRM practices, much remains to be done in the field.

This paper reviews the discussions and conclusions reached at the conference "Research for Relevance in International Management" with regard to future directions for IHRM research. This paper is based on ideas presented by the workshop leader, Rosalie Tung, supplemented by group discussions[1] which took place over a two-day period. The discussions were wide-ranging; hence it is not possible to cover every aspect of them, rather, the main points are summarized. It is hoped that this review will provide academics with ideas regarding potentially relevant research projects in IHRM. Peterson (1988) suggested that "it would be great if every person who participated in the conference picked up one idea for a proposal for future research"; this review should serve to encourage those

[1] The authors would like to thank the following participants in the conference group for their valuable contributions to this paper: Colette Frayne, University of Western Ontario; Yitzak Fried, Wayne State University; Rabi Kanungo, McGill University; Andre Laurent, INSEAD; Mark Mendenhall, University of Tennessee-Chattanooga; and Richard Peterson, Washington University.

who participated, as well as those who did not, to identify specific research projects which meet the criteria of relevance.

5.2 Future Directions for IHRM Research

5.2.1 Criteria for Relevant IHRM Research

The following points summarize the criteria for relevant IHRM research, as developed by the group:

5.2.1.1 Need for Theory Development

Currently, there is a lack of IHRM theory. In order to advance, we need to develop theoretical frameworks from which hypotheses can be generated and tested. To develop theories will necessitate engaging in exploratory research and confronting all of the problems associated with exploratory research. In addition, theories may be borrowed initially from related, more established areas.

5.2.1.2 Need for Different Perspectives

Relevant IHRM research will incorporate multiple perspectives. This means developing projects which build in the unique perspectives of the MNC management, the nation, and the academic researcher as part of the research design.

5.2.1.3 Need for Multiple Levels of Relevance

In order to be truly useful and usable, IHRM research will need to be concerned with its relevance to multiple constituencies, including the MNC, the strategic alliance partners, and the practitioner-consultant, in addition to the academic researcher.

5.2.1.4 Need to Consider Management of Change

Perhaps the single most important challenge for IHRM is the management of change. The academic researcher needs to be cognizant that IHRM is often practised in organizational contexts undergoing change, e.g., in new and evolving strategic alliances, in expanding MNC's, and in tenuously forged international joint ventures. The issues for the international manager revolve around adaptation: career development for foreign assignments, repatriation, and integration of a multicultural workforce.

5.2.1.5 Need to Understand Strategic Alliances

International strategic alliances bring together HRM systems which may have both similarities and differences. Very much needed is research which focuses on the merging of HRM practices, how this is managed, and the impact on both the managers and the workers. In addition, strategic alliances raise the issue of the need for totally new HRM practices.

5.2.1.6 Need for Alternative Research Sites

As a follow-up to the above point, a first step may be to investigate those organizations identified as having advanced IHRM practices. Additionally, IHRM researchers may gain new perspectives by conducting research in alternative organizational sites which have a long history of international operations, namely, the foreign services (e.g, diplomatic missions, the Peace Corps, and United Nations missions) and international non-profit organizations (e.g., Amnesty International, Save the Children, and the International Red Cross).

5.2.1.7 Need for Alternative Research Directions

One criticism of IHRM is that it has not been sufficiently diverse or innovative in its approaches, concentrating on surveys, interviews, and observations. As a result, the body of knowledge is restrictive. Some alternative research directions may be historical studies, comparative studies of management practices, and translation of foreign HRM literature.

5.2.1.8 Internationalization of the Workplace

A recognized but under-researched phenomenon is the internationalization of the workplace. Some relevant topics to be pursued are: culture and its effect on behavior in organizations; internationalization of top management; and the multi-ethnic workforce.

The wide variety of potential research projects in IHRM makes it difficult to choose among them and to limit projects appropriately. To guide the development of future research projects, a framework was developed at the conference to incorporate some of the main ideas discussed. While a wide variety of dimensions and categories within each dimension could have been used to define such a framework, the model proposed (see Figure 5.1) incorporated those variables which were considered to be most relevant to the current issues of IHRM.

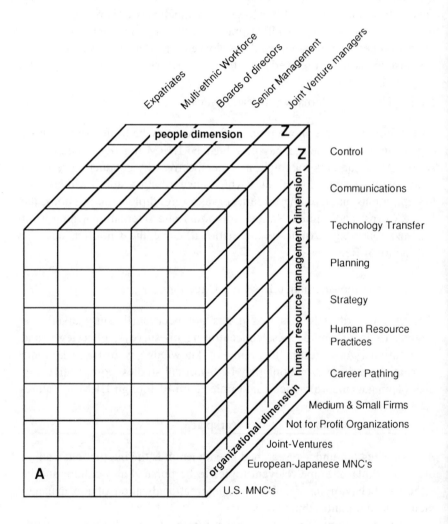

Figure 5.1 *Framework for specifying international management research projects*

This model identifies three dimensions: type of international organization (organizational dimension), area of human resource management (HRM dimension), and persons or positions in the organization (people dimension). Within each dimension a number of categories are represented. Organizational types included are: U.S. MNC's, European-Japanese MNC's, joint-ventures, Not-for-Profit firms, and medium and small firms. The people dimension is comprised of: expatriates, multi-ethnic workforces, boards of directors, senior management, and joint-venture managers. The human resource management dimension includes issues of: control, communication, transfer of technology, planning, strategy, human resource practices, and career-pathing. The model proposes that the intersection of these three dimensions provides a means of specifying research projects. For example, Cell A in Figure 5.1 identifies research focusing on the career-pathing of expatriates in U.S. MNC's; Cell Z focuses on control.

5.3 General Research Frameworks

Two general frameworks may be particularly appropriate to the investigation of IHRM practices. These are briefly summarized below:

5.3.1 International Organizational Development Model

This is based on the concept that organizations fit into one of three phases, essentially paralleling the Product Life Cycle Model (Vernon, 1966; see especially: Adler and Ghadar, Chapter 6). Briefly, this model suggests the following:

1. A Phase One firm focuses on the home market and is concerned with adapting its product or service to the home market; foreign markets, as they develop, are served by exports;
2. A Phase Two firm moves operations abroad to be close to foreign markets and serves each foreign location individually;
3. The Phase Three firm serves all markets, including the home market from a limited number of locations chosen for their efficiency.

These phases might be used to provide a framework for examining the issues raised above; i.e. a contingency approach to IHRM could be developed in terms of the three phases and firms representing the various phases could be empirically investigated. For example, one hypothesis might be that staffing practices would vary from phase to phase. Effective firms in the first phase would use home country managers almost exclusively; in the second phase they would use host country managers; and in the third phase they would take a geocentric approach to staffing (using the best manager for a particular job regardless of national origin). Similarly, selection techniques, appropriate training, length of foreign assignments, and other such factors might be related to organizational phase.

This approach is appealing, but a number of issues need to be considered in this context:

1. Each phase needs to be identified as discrete, and firms tracked through them. Operational variables need to be identified and measured.
2. It may be difficult to categorize an entire organization in these terms, particularly because different parts of the organization may be operating at different phases of the cycle.
3. Local differences in HRM practices should be taken into account. It is likely that situational variables encountered in different locations may affect an organization's choice of HRM practices and these would have to be incorporated into the model. For example, the model might predict a polycentric staffing approach but local laws may proscribe the use of a large number of foreigners.
4. IHRM practices which change in response to these phases should be differentiated from those that remain constant. It seems likely that certain practices, for example, short term foreign assignments for technical specialists, would remain the same through all phases of the cycle. Others, such as the use of local personnel in top positions, would be more likely to change in response to different phases.
5. A dynamic model should be developed and investigated by looking at organizations in transition, i.e. as they are moving from one phase to another. This could be related to changes in IHRM practices and organizational success. A proactive role for IHRM could thus be identified within this framework.

5.3.2 Historical Perspective Model

An analysis of the development of IHRM practices over time could provide valuable insight into effective management of human resources internationally. Such an approach would examine IHRM practices of international companies from different home countries and in different host countries. The evolution of IHRM approaches would be examined and related to some measure of their apparent effectiveness. This approach is interesting, but the following questions need to be considered:

5.3.2.1 Are Adequate Data Available to Identify the Evolution of IHRM Practices over Time?

There are sources of archival data such as case studies, company records, historical company descriptions, but these are not always easy to locate. The World Federation of Personnel Managers Association was suggested as a possible source of comparative historical human resource information.

5.3.2.2 What Operational Variables Would Be Investigated?

To illustrate the challenge of deciding which variables will be considered, following are a few that might be appropriate – staffing practices, selection and training practices, management mix (parent country, host country, third country), length of foreign assignments, success/failure of foreign assignments, the role of women in foreign locations, fit of corporate and local culture, subsidiary/joint venture corporate culture.

5.3.2.3 How Would Effectiveness Be Defined and Measured?

Effectiveness is not easily identified because it needs to incorporate the viewpoint of a variety of different stakeholders; including, among others, the owners, the employees, the managers, the public, the host government, the home government, customers, suppliers, creditors. Generally, effectiveness is associated with satisfaction with an entity's performance on the part of the major stakeholders. Measuring satisfaction is often difficult, particularly where different stakeholders may react differently. Typically, evidence of profitability, longevity, employee, customer, supplier satisfaction are used to indicate effectiveness.

5.3.2.4 How Would Effectiveness Be Clearly Related to IHRM Practices?

In order to relate effectiveness to IHRM practices, control for other variables (economic, financial, technological, legal, etc.) which might influence effectiveness would be very important.

5.3.2.5 How Would Country Differences (e.g., Cultural, Legal, Political) Be Related to Differences in IHRM Practices?

The possible effect of these variables needs to be identified prior to undertaking research in order to track their influence on the relationships under investigation.

In summary, in order to track the historical development of IHRM and reach conclusions regarding the most appropriate IHRM practices, research projects need to be very carefully designed. The variables to be investigated should be carefully thought out and justified; equally, control for extraneous variables must be built into the design of the project. This type of research, well done, provides many interesting and exciting opportunities for the IHRM investigator.

5.4 Status of the Field

As noted by the conference group participants, the status of IHRM research is quite underdeveloped at this time. This makes the field of IHRM an exciting one from a research perspective because much remains to be investigated. However, it is clear that substantial progress will be made only if there is a clear definition of what constitutes IHRM. IHRM researchers should, therefore, be careful to clearly identify and define the variables to be investigated in any research. Given the relatively underdeveloped state of theory in the field, it may be appropriate to borrow from other established disciplines as well as engage in exploratory and descriptive research.

There appears to be a consensus that the first priorities are a clear definition of IHRM and theory development leading to the identification of some specific questions for investigation. These include the following.

1. What is meant by IHRM? What is it that is going to be studied?
2. What is known about IHRM? What do companies actually do?
3. Which IHRM practices are universal? Which are peculiar to specific locations and times?

4. How can IHRM practices be related to organizational effective-ness? Do IHRM practices actually have an impact on performan-ce/success?

While more exploratory and descriptive research needs to be done to better understand IHRM practices, this does not imply that future research can be less rigorous. In contrast, well-designed and rigorous research is the key to developing well-grounded theories in the area; these can sub-sequently lead to the formulation of useful conceptual frameworks and practical approaches for managers. Relevant research implies careful con-sideration, understanding and integration of practitioners' needs as well as academic concerns.

5.4.1 Incorporating Practitioners Needs into Research

The following section briefly summarizes a number of specific research projects suggested as examples which incorporate practitioners' needs.

5.4.1.1 Consideration of the Impact of International Assignments on Managerial Careers

The continuing need for managers to serve in foreign locations suggests that this would be an issue of concern to management in international organizations. The suggested methodology was questionnaires followed by interviews. Questionnaires would provide a relatively large response set, and interviews would serve to clarify and supplement the information gathered in a survey.

5.4.3.2 Examination of the Human Side of Strategic Alliances and the Impact of Blending of Two Sets of HRM Practices

The increasing number of international strategic alliances suggests that this issue will be of concern to international organizations. The suggested methodology would identify and compare two contrasting sets of compa-nies: one set where HRM practices were specifically considered as part of the strategic alliance, the other set where HRM practices were not considered. Hypotheses would be developed and investigated regarding the relationship of HRM considerations and measures of effectiveness, such as turnover, productivity, and satisfaction. This approach would cla-rify the importance of HRM considerations for international companies.

5.4.3.3 Comparison of Successful and Unsuccessful HRM Practices in Various Locations, for Example, at Home, in Subsidiaries and in Strategic Alliances

Identification of specific approaches that are effective in different locations would provide practical guidance for managers designing HRM systems for international organizations. The suggested methodology was a series of case studies examining different approaches in different locations. Such a set of case studies would allow for an in-depth examination of the different approaches in a realistic setting.

5.4.3.4 Investigation of a Small Number of Executives Who Consider International Experience Important to Identify Why They Developed this Attitude

This would help bridge the apparent gap between academics who believe international experience is critical to management effectiveness and managers who consider it of lesser importance. The methodology suggested was to identify executives initially through a survey then to conduct in-depth unstructured interviews with each executive. The survey would serve to identify those executives who do consider international experience important while the unstructured interview process would allow a wide variety of reasons to be identified and explored in detail.

5.4.3.5 Identification of HRM Practices in Use in Different Countries and the Objectives that they are Intended to Accomplish

This would serve to provide location-specific guidance for international organizations which should be of practical importance. The methodology suggested was a survey, possibly through the World Federation of Personnel Management Association, to identify current practices worldwide. This could be followed by interviews with selected representatives of top management and HRM executives in various countries to corroborate the information from the survey.

5.5 Future Research Considerations

In her opening address at the conference, Tung identified six specific aspects of IHRM as deserving further attention. These are: communication and control in multinationals, management of human resources in international cooperative ventures, relating international human resource management to the overall strategic management framework in the company, management of a multi-ethnic workforce, use of dual-career couples in international assignments and repatriation.

Clearly, there is a need for extensive research in the field of IHRM. What is less clear is how this research can be made relevant. This question was redirected at the conference as "relevance for whom?". The consensus is that there are two important perspectives to consider in terms of relevance: the practitioner's, whose concern is immediate and problem-oriented, and the academic's concern, which is longer-term and knowledge-oriented.

If research is to be relevant, both perspectives need to be taken into account. The difficulty is that the two often seem to be in conflict. The practitioner is concerned with the day-to-day decisions of dealing with employees from a variety of countries, within the context of the organization's objectives. The academic, in contrast, is often concerned with broader issues of effective human resource management, and these may be neither organization-specific nor situation-specific.

In order to deal with this apparent conflict, academics can take a leading role. They can develop conceptual frameworks and test IHRM practices to identify those that are most effective in different circumstances. This approach builds on the academics' concern with broader issues while providing the information for daily decisions needed by the practitioners.

While it is desirable to integrate the concerns and interests of both academics and practitioners, there may be problems of implementation. A number of issues surface in an attempt to clarify needed action on the part of IHRM researchers. These are summarized below:

1. There is a lack of understanding of the context of IHRM; therefore, there is a need to define the nature of the problems faced in IHRM and to specify what is meant by IHRM.

2. There is a lack of well-defined theory in IHRM; therefore, much exploratory research is needed in the field to develop appropriate conceptual frameworks.

3. There is an almost infinite variety in organization approaches to IHRM; therefore, there is a need to provide a conceptual framework within which to examine each unique context.

4. There is an overlap between IHRM and many other disciplines (e.g., anthropology, industrial and organizational psychology, organiza-

tional behavior, political science, sociology); therefore, IHRM needs to build on research that has been done in other areas.

5. There are at least two perspectives that need to be considered in IHRM: that of the organization (often an MNC) and that of the host country; therefore, research should consider effectiveness from both points of view.

6. There is a tendency to be parochial in North American research; therefore, it is important to realize that practitioners and academics in other countries can provide North Americans with useful and enlightening information.

5.5.1 Specific Research Agendas

To provide some illustrations of specific research projects which incorporate the concerns raised above, this section discusses in more detail the six aspects of IHRM identified by Tung.

5.5.1.1 Communication and Control in Multinational Corporations

To meet the localization policies of many host societies and to reduce the high cost associated with expatriation, more host country nationals are used in staffing overseas subsidiaries. In her study of IHRM, Tung (1989) found that U.S. multinationals tend to use host country nationals extensively at the senior, middle and lower management levels in their European, Canadian, Australian and New Zealand operations. Host country nationals were also widely used at the middle and lower management levels in their Latin American and Far Eastern subsidiaries.

While the advantages associated with the use of host country nationals are manifold, such as reduced cost and better relations with the host country, the policy of localization does pose problems of communication and control between the subsidiary and parent headquarters and among sister affiliates. In their book, *The Multinational Mission* (1987), Prahalad and Doz identified the dilemma that multinational corporations have to contend with, namely, the need for global integration, on the one hand, and the need for local responsiveness, on the other.

To meet these challenges, multinationals have to develop a set of strategies which can manage effectively the complexities and dynamics of such communication and control procedures. These developments also have important implications for international human resource management in terms of staffing requirements and of developing personnel to meet the dual objectives of global integration and local responsiveness.

5.5.1.2   Management of Human Resource in International Cooperative Ventures

An emerging trend in the game of global economic competition is global alliances. These cooperative agreements take one or more of several forms, such as joint ventures, co-marketing, co-production and joint research and development.

Some of the most successful multinationals have pursued this strategy. Industry giants such as IBM, Boeing, General Motors, Nippon Telegraph and Telephone and Phillips, which were once averse to cooperative ventures with other entities, whether domestic or international, have now entered into such alliances. In 1985 and 1986, it was estimated that more than 1,000 cooperative agreements were signed between U.S. and European companies. In a May 18, 1987 article in *Business Week,* entitled, "Hands Across Europe: Joint Ventures will help Companies Compete against Japan and the U.S.", it profiled the wave of mergers that swept Europe. The article went on to state: "There are signs . . . that the old bugaboo of each country, insisting on having its 'national champion' in sexy high-tech areas is breaking down". With the 1992 Single Europe Act, these consolidations will further increase.

Cooperative ventures and cross-national acquisitions pose special challenges to companies and require that human resource management planning and practices be revised to accommodate this new calculus in global economic cooperation and competition. For example, how does one merge and manage the differences in management philosophies and systems between entities from two separate countries?

5.5.1.3   Relating International Human Resource Management to the Overall Strategic Management Framework in the Company

In most U.S. companies, human resource management has been traditionally de-emphasized. In the 1984 book, *Key to Japan's Economic Strength: Human Power,* Tung hypothesized that one of the reasons for the decline in U.S. international competitiveness is the lack of emphasis on international human resource management. In the past, the United States has relied on technology to gain the competitive edge. With the narrowing technological gap between the United States, Japan and Europe, U.S. multinationals can no longer rely solely on technology to gain a competitive edge in international markets. Rather, their focus should be shifted to the area of human resource planning because companies and technology are, after all, managed and operated by people.

According to a report in the *Wall Street Journal* (October 18, 1988:A1), human resource managers in an increasing number of U.S. companies are beginning to assume greater stature in their respective corporate hierarchies. Reasons cited for such changes were: "cost control, increased competition, more complex wage and benefits, and new needs of a changing workforce".

Studies should examine how human resource management can be integrated into the overall framework of corporate strategic planning and management.

5.5.1.4 Management of a Multi-Ethnic Workforce

According to the Hudson Institute, the U.S. workforce has undergone and will continue to undergo tremendous and rapid changes in terms of its demographic profile. In 1985, for example, the composition of the U.S. work force was as follows: 47% U.S. born white males, 36% U.S. born white females, 5% each of U.S. born non-white male and U.S. born non-white females, 4% immigrant males, and 3% immigrant females. This profile is expected to change dramatically within the next fifteen years. Between 1985 and 2000, it was projected that the profile of new entrants to the labor force will be as follows: 15% U.S. born white males, 42% U.S. born white females, 7% U.S. born non-white males, 13% U.S. born non-white females, 13% immigrant males, and 10% immigrant females (*Business Week*, September 19, 1988).

This change in composition of the workforce and the increasing diversity of ethnic backgrounds of new entrants pose special challenges to companies, both domestic and international. Studies should examine how human resource management planning and practices ought to be revised in light of these changes.

5.5.1.5 Use of Dual-Career Couples in International Assignments

In a survey of directors of human resource management of 20 U.S. multinationals, the majority believed that the issue of dual-career families will be a major problem confronting their companies in the next decade (Tung, 1988b). This issue may not be as imminent in other countries. In Japan, for example, because most Japanese wives do not work outside of their home, the issue of dual-career couples may not be a concern among Japanese multinationals. In both Europe and Australia, while many women work, this problem is less pressing because of the lower percentage of women who are employed as professionals in these countries.

In the United States, two-income families have become an increasingly common phenomenon in the recent past. In 1986, the number of two-income families reached 22.6 million as compared to 13.9 million in 1967 (U.S. Department of Labor). Furthermore, an increasing percentage of women are entering into the professions. In fact, approximately 40 % of students currently enrolled in MBA programs across North American business schools are women.

The problem of relocation of dual-career couples is not unique to international assignments. While the deployment of dual-career couples within the domestic context is difficult, this problem tends to be magnified several-fold across national boundaries for two primary reasons. First is the problem of work permit restrictions in some host societies. Countries such as the United States, Australia, and Switzerland seldom grant work permits to both spouses unless they possess expertise and skills which are in short supply. In some countries, while there are no work permit restrictions, there may be a strong bias against women working in predominantly male occupations. Second is the difficulty of keeping both careers on track while abroad. At some multinationals, couples have to decide quite early in their careers which of the two will have the lead career. One spouse will have to make career sacrifices and his/her career will then trail behind the other. This is no easy decision and imposes extra strains on a marital relationship (Tung, 1988a).

Many multinationals seemed to be of the opinion that the relocation of dual-career couples is a family or personal matter; consequently, the company should basically adopt a "hands-off" policy. While few employees welcome company interference into their personal lives and affairs, the issue of relocation of dual-career couples is not entirely a personal matter. Because of the magnitude of the problem, the company should offer active assistance to the couple for resolving this dilemma.

The contention is made that given the importance of the global economy, it is imperative that organizations develop an international orientation among its candidates for senior management. If one assumes that dual-career couples have high professional aspirations, and there appears to be support for this contention, they are the employees who eventually will rise to the top ranks of management. Consequently, it is very important for people in such key positions to have international exposure. This international perspective can be acquired through one or two stints of offshore assignments. However, unless couples and companies can resolve some of the issues associated with the deployment of dual-career couples of international assignments, such as finding jobs for working spouses, more and more managers will refuse international assignments. In fact, in seminars conducted by Tung with MBA students from several business schools on the specific subject, many felt that if their companies were reluctant to provide assistance in this matter, they would opt out from the corporate world and set up their own businesses. One corporate reaction to the difficulties posed by dual-career couples was to look outside of North America for its international managers (Punnett, 1989). This has serious implications for the quality and orientation of the people who will manage American corporations in the future and, consequently, for U.S. competitiveness in the world market in the twenty-first century. Research should help identify strategies for the deployment of dual-career couples in international assignments.

5.5.1.6 Repatriation

A full 57% of the U.S. multinationals identified repatriation as one of the most critical challenges in the area of IHRM in the decade ahead (Tung, 1989). The issues associated with repatriation are essentially two-fold: career advancement opportunities and relocation upon return (Tung, 1988b). Why do these problems exist? This situation derives from the fact that while companies may expend effort on the expatriation side to facilitate adaptation to the foreign environmental setting, such as the provision of pre-departure training and other types of relocation assistance, including the finding of accommodation, most U.S. corporations often do little for the individual upon repatriation because it is assumed that the problems of reentry to the home country and home operation are minimal.

Unfortunately, this is not always true because the process of reentry to the home office and home country after several years of absence may be traumatic. Problems include settling into a new position, purchasing a home, and the spouse's searching for a new job. Research has shown that expatriates and their families often experience a reverse culture shock upon reentry (Harvey, 1982; Piet-Pelon and Hornby, 1986). The reentry process can be particularly painful when expectations of upward career advancement are not realized. Frustration sets in when the repatriate finds that he/she is not able to utilize immediately the skills and experience acquired abroad.

This phenomenon is relatively common among U.S. multinationals where an international experience is not considered a very important criterion for promotion to senior management positions. In a study by Tung and Miller (1988) of management succession policies in 123 U.S. companies, the majority of which had annual gross operating revenues in excess of $1 billion, over 93 % of the respondents did not consider "international experience or perspective" as one of the five most important criteria for promotion/recruitment into the ranks of senior management. In comparison, given their smaller domestic markets, European, Japanese and Australian multinationals generally place a high premium on the experience and skills acquired overseas (Tung, 1988b).

In many U.S. multinationals, some repatriates may even find that their career progression has stagnated as compared with that of their peers who have remained home. In fact, some high achievers refuse an overseas assignment for fear that it may result in a negative career move. According to a 1987 survey by Moran, Stahl and Boyer Inc., a consulting firm in Colorado, only 4 % of the U.S. companies surveyed considered overseas assignments as having "a positive effect on career advancement" (*Wall Street Journal*, June 30, 1987). This practice stands in stark contrast to the policies espoused by many leading European, Japanese and Australian multinationals (Tung, 1988b). In the majority of European, Japanese and Australian multinationals, an overseas assignment, particularly one to a major financial or commercial center of the world, is viewed as a strong cue for subsequent promotion in the organization. For example, it is generally known that the person who will ultimately assume the position of chairman of the board of a leading Japanese general trading company must have served in the firm's New York or London operation. According to the executive of a major Australian bank, "If a person was selected for an offshore assignment, he had struck it rich, he had cracked the jackpot".

What accounts for this difference in attitude toward an international assignment among U.S., European, Japanese and Australian multinationals? The factors appear to be two-fold. One, the majority of European, Japanese and Australian companies derive a significantly larger proportion of their corporate revenues from abroad. As such, positions abroad are often viewed as exciting and challenging. As an executive of a large Swiss multinational explained, "It doesn't mean that the jobs (in corporate headquarters) are unimportant, but it puts a somewhat different tenor on where the important jobs are" (Tung, 1988a). As noted earlier, in most of the European, Japanese and Australian multinationals, international experience is considered as an important requisite for promotion to top management. To quote the executive of National Westminster Bank, a major U.K. financial institution, "It is known throughout the company that once a person is selected for an overseas assignment, 99 percent of the time it is a promotion" (Tung, 1988b:242).

A second factor which has accounted for this difference in attitude is the prevalence of the "out-of-sight, out-of-mind" syndrome among many U.S. multinationals. Because of the heavier emphasis assigned to domestic operations, many people fear that if they were removed from corporate headquarters for an extended period of time, they would be out of the mainstream and hence might be bypassed in the promotion process within the corporate organizational hierarchy. According to an executive at Unilever, a European conglomerate:

> The thing which gives expatriate experience a bad reputation faster than anything else is poor reabsorption or reintegration back into the mainstream in the home country. The money issue can be coped with; teaching them the language can also be dealt with – you can teach them all those things. But you won't win even if you do all of them right, if they see that the last person who came back was worse off than when he left. Every time there is a casualty, it gets magnified more than a hundred-fold. Like everything in life, everybody knows about the casualty. They forget about all the ones that were successful. You do damage most quickly by bad onward career progression (Tung, 1988a).

In an article in the *Academy of Management Executive* Tung (1988b) examined the career issues of international assignments and offered suggestions on how multinationals can cope with these problems.

5.6 Conclusion

In conclusion, changes in the calculus of global economic cooperation and competition and the composition of the labor force, suggest that international human resource management policies and practices which have served us well in the past will prove to be inadequate in the future. In light of these changes, researchers have to work hand-in-hand with practitioners to identify the strategic challenges that face the planning and management of international human resources in the decades ahead and, more importantly, to develop a set of recommendations to meet these challenges.

5.7 References

Harvey, M.C. (1982). The Other Side of Foreign Assignments: Dealing with the Repatriation Dilemma, *Columbia Journal of World Business,* Spring, 53–59.

Peterson, R. (1988). Letter to B.J. Punnett, 1.

Piet-Pelon, N.J. and B. Hornby (1986). *Women Overseas.* Exeter, U.K.: A Wheaton & Co.

Prahalad, C.K. and Y.L. Doz (1987). *The Multinational Mission,* New York: The Free Press.

Punnett, B.J. (1989). Human Resource Management in International Canadian Companies. In A. Rugman (ed.), *Canadian Dimensions of International Business: A Strategic Approach.* Toronto: Prentice-Hall Canada, 330–346.

Tung, R. L. (1984). *Key to Japan's Economic Strength: Human Power,* Lexington, MA: Lexington Books.

Tung, R. L., (1988a). *The New Expatriates: Managing Human Resources Abroad,* Cambridge, MA: Ballinger.

Tung, R. L., (1988b). Career Issues in International Assignments. *Academy of Management Executive,* Volume 2, No. 3, 241–244.

Tung, R. L., and E. L. Miller (1988). Managing in the Twenty-first Century: The Need for Global Orientation. Paper presented at the Annual Meeting of the Academy of International Business, San Diego, CA, Oct. 20–23.

Tung, R. L. (1989). International Assignments: Strategic Challenges in the 21st Century. Paper presented at the 49th Annual Meeting of the Academy of Management, Washington, D.C., August 14–16.

Vernon, R. (1966). International Investment and International Trade the Product Cycle. *Quarterly Journal of Economics,* May, 190–207.

6 A Strategic Phase Approach to International Human Resources Management[1]

Nancy J. Adler
McGill University
Fariborz Ghadar
George Washington University

6.1 Introduction

In this chapter, we ask three fundamental questions. First, as a context for addressing human resource management issues, what is the evolution of the multinational enterprise and, most predictably, where will it go from here? Second, does national culture affect the firm and thereby its management of people, and third, what are the implications of the firm's evolution for the effective management of people?

One of the central questions facing international human resource professionals is the influence, or lack thereof, of culture on the management of people worldwide. Discussions concerning the influence of culture on strategic efficacy remain time-lagged and disconnected from other corporate realities. Scholars and managers alike continue to ask if culture impacts organizational functioning rather than, more relevantly, when, or under what conditions does it do so? Perhaps the field would be more successful if it made its inquiry within the context of the evolving strategies and structures of global firms, rather than confining it to the more static assumptions that have governed international personnel decision for years. What, then, are the implications of the phase of the firm's evolution for effectively managing people?

---

[1] This chapter is partially based on Nancy J. Adler and Fariborz Ghadar's (1990) work reported in "Strategic Human Resource Management: A Global Perspective", in Rüdiger Pieper (ed.), Human Resource Management in International Comparison. Berlin/New York: de Gruyter, 235–260.

6.2 Global Strategy from the Perspective of Culture

This chapter focuses on global strategy from the perspective of culture and the management of people. It uses the development of American multinationals as a base, starting with the product life cycle in international trade and investment and proceeding to a commonly accepted three-phase model[2] describing the evolution of multinational enterprises (MNE's) from World War II to the present. Then, going beyond the third phase, it outlines some of the possible characteristics of future phase four MNE's. Within this framework of the evolving multinational firm, the chapter suggests some new and more powerful approaches to managing human resource systems and the cultural diversity engendered in global operations.

6.2.1 The Model

One way that has been used to understand the evolution of international firms is through the products they produce. In the United States and Canada, post World War II economic conditions played a determining role in the way business approached the development, manufacturing, and marketing of products. Vernon (1966) observed that one could divide the international product life cycle for trade and investment into three principal phases: high tech, growth and internationalization, and maturity. As shown in Table 6.1, these form the basis of a three-phase development model for multinational enterprises.

6.2.1.1 Phase One: A Product Orientation

The salient characteristic of Phase One's products is that they are new and unique. Only a handful of companies are capable of developing and manufacturing any specific product. These new products are purchased by a highly specialized and limited market. Given their uniqueness and the few companies capable of producing them, Phase One products generally command a high price relative to direct costs.

---

[2] While originally espoused by Vernon in 1966, this argument has been picked up by many commentators; also see (Vernon, 1971, 1981), Ghadar (1977, 1985, 1986), among others, and more recently, Bartlett and Ghoshal, (1989).

Table 6.1 *The International Product Life Cycle*

	Phase I Domestic Start-up	Phase II Growth & Internation-alization	Phase III Multination-alization	Phase IV Globalization
Competitive Strategy	Domestic	Multidomestic	Multinational	Global
Importance of International	Marginal	Important	Dominant	Continual
Primary Orientation	Product	Market	Price	Strategy
Product	New, unique & non-standard	More standardized	Completely standardized	Mass customized
Manufacturing Location	Domestic production	Driven by market size	Determined by produc-tion costs	Determined by produc-tion costs

6.2.1.2 Phase Two: A Market Orientation

The entrance of competition marks the beginning of Phase Two, growth and internationalization. Initially, the firm supplies new foreign markets through exports from the home country. As these foreign markets grow, more is produced locally and exports from the original home country begin to diminish.

Market penetration and control replace research and development as the most important functions because the product technology has been refined in Phase One. Moreover, with other firms continuing to enter the market as producers, competition increases and drives down both price and the ratio of price to cost.

6.2.1.3 Phase Three: A Price Orientation

Products enter Phase Three when competition forces standardization of the production process. Standardization continues in Phase Three until further reductions in production costs become impossible. Due to the competition, price often falls to a bare minimum above cost. Phase Three firms can gain a competitive advantage only by shifting production to those countries in which the elements of production are least expensive. Production costs, rather than market consideration, determine location, and even the home country market may be supplied primarily by production imported from offshore plants.

6.2.1.4 The Accelerated Product Life Cycle

In the years immediately following the Second World War, products developed by North American companies took between fifteen and twenty years to move through the international product life cycle described above. However, by the the 1970's, its acceleration made the need for new strategies and models, and thus for new kinds of multinational enterprises imminent. By the 1980's, the development cycle for many products and services had been shortened to three to five years. For some products and services, it now takes less than six months. While the dramatic changes in strategy, structure, production and marketing have been evident, the changes affect human resource management systems have been considerably less clear.

6.2.1.5 The Future: A Possible Phase Four

Stan Davis, in his book *Future Perfect* (1987) tells us that we are entering an era of mass customization, in which products are designed to meet individual needs while their components will be sourced and assembled worldwide. Successful firms will be globally responsive: that is, they will listen to clients, accurately identify trends, and respond quickly.

To succeed in such a Phase Four environment, firms must become simultaneously more highly differentiated and more integrated. Structurally, successful firms will have passed far beyond the international divisions and foreign subsidiaries of Phase Two as well as the global lines of business of Phase Three, to global heterarchies[3] (Hedlund, 1986) that weave together complex networks of joint ventures, wholly-owned subsidiaries and organi-

---

[3] Heterarchies, as used by Gunnar Hedlund (1986), describe non-hierarchically organized systems: e.g., holographic coding where entire systems are represented or "known" within each component of the system.

zational and project defined alliances (Galbraith and Kazanjian, 1986). Managers in this type of environment will use multifocal approaches combining Phase Two's demands for increased local responsiveness with Phase Three's opportunities for global integration (Doz and Prahalad, 1986; Adler and Bartholomew, 1992b). To maintain responsiveness, successful firms will develop global corporate cultures that recognize cultural diversity and its impact on the organization (Adler and Jelinek, 1986), thus allowing them to integrate culture-specific strategic choices within a global vision of the firm (Laurent, 1986). Appropriate approaches to human resource management in these types of cooperative ventures will have to be redefined (Lorange, 1986).

6.3   The Consequences of Culture

How important are cultural differences to international organizational effectiveness? As indicated in Table 6.2, the importance of cultural differences depends on the phase of the life cycle in which the firm operates. Because Phase One firms produce unique products that they offer primarily to their own domestic market, they can appropriately operate from an ethnocentric perspective and ignore most cultural differences they encounter.

As Phase Two competition brings the need to market and to produce abroad, sensitivity to cultural differences becomes critical to implementing an effective corporate strategy. As Phase One's product orientation shifts to Phase Two's marketing orientation, the firm must address each foreign market separately.

As firms enter Phase Three, the environment again changes and with it the demands for cultural sensitivity. By Phase Three, many firms produce the same, almost undifferentiated product and therefore firms compete almost exclusively on price. This price competition reduces the importance of most cross-cultural differences along with almost any advantage the firm could have gained by sensitivity to them.

By Phase Four, top-quality, least-possible-cost products and services become the minimally acceptable standard. Competitive advantage comes from sophisticated global strategies based on mass customization. One of the critical components on which Phase Four firms segment the market again becomes culture. Successful firms understand their potential clients' worldwide needs, quickly translate them into products and services, produce those products and services on a least-possible-cost basis, and deliver them back to the client in a culturally appropriate and timely fashion.

Table 6.2 *A Cultural Perspective on the International Product Life Cycle*

	Phase I Domestic Start-up	Phase II Growth & Internation- alization	Phase III Multination- alization	Phase IV Globalization
Perspective	Ethnocentric	Polycentric or regiocentric	Multinational	Global- multicentric
Cultural Sensitivity	Unimportant	Critically important	Marginally Important	Very important
Primary Pro- duct Design and Market Assumption	"One-way" or "one-best way"	Equifinality or "many- best ways"	"One-least- cost way"	Many simultaneous best ways
Typical Organizational Structure	Centralized- functional divisions	Country sales offices; then international division	Global lines of business	Global heterarchy

6.4 International Human Resource Management

International human resource management (IHRM) involves the worldwide management of people (see: Tung, 1984 and Miller et al., 1986, among
others). The following section describes the approaches to managing people which best fit each phase in the firm's development (Table 6.3). It
provides a framework for understanding the effectiveness of each approach based on the match between the internal characteristic of the firm's
human system and the external business requirements for interaction with
foreign economies. The framework outlines the ideal degree of internationalization of the human resource system based on the firm's phase of
business and strategic development.

There are two direct applications of the framework described here.
First, the model predicts the criteria for successful international staffing
at each phase of the organization's development. Second, the model also
predicts IHRM problems encountered by firms in each phase which reflect

the mismatch of personnel selection, skills, and training to the requirements of that phase. In general, North American firms have not fully recognized the shifts in personnel requirements as they make the transition from one phase to the next (see Adler and Bartholomew, 1992b). As a result, they continue to recruit and train international managers based on the success criteria of previous phases.

Table 6.3 *The Phase Model Applied to International Human Resource Management*

	Phase I Domestic Start-up	Phase II Growth & Inernation-alization	Phase III Multination-alization	Phase IV Globalization
Staffing Selection	No expatriates	Many expatriates	Some Ex-patriates and Inpatriates	Many ex-patriates, in-patriates and transpatriates
Who sent	Marketing people	Marketing people, country director financial officer technical experts	Country directors and financial officers as expatrates, high potential managers as inpatriates	High potential managers and top executives
Purpose of Assignment	To get job done	To get job done	To get job done and career development	To get job done, career development, & organizatio-nal integration
Career Impact and Re-entry	Bad for career Somewhat difficult	Bad for dome-stic career Extremely difficult	Important for global career Less difficult	Essential to reach executi-ve suite Professionally easy

6.4.1 Phase One

In Phase One, the firm produces a unique product and sells it primarily to its own domestic market. Given this domestic focus and the absence of competition, the firm's needs for internationally sophisticated people are minimal. This monopoly situation forces potential buyers (rather than the seller) to absorb the cross-cultural mismatches. Foreign buyers must speak the language and accept business practices appropriate to the firm's home environment. At the same time, buyers must alter the products and services, once purchased, to fit their needs. Not surprisingly, the majority of firms operating under Phase One assumptions provide no cross-cultural or pre-departure training for any of their employees or managers.

From a research perspective, the degree of multiculturalism or foreign expertise of the management has little relation to the firm's effectiveness. Similarly, in Phase One, foreign language capability and other international skills would rarely be considered an asset nor would an international assignment be helpful in advancing individuals in their careers.

6.4.1.1 Criteria for Phase One IHRM

Since domestic sales have traditionally accounted for most Phase One profits, firms generally do not assign their best people to the few international positions. In selecting people for international travel, the firm's primary consideration is "getting the job done". This is true, for example, for technical expertise. Neither international career development for the employee nor international organizational development for the firm is considered important because international is not important, as reported in Chapter Five (Tung and Punnett). Consequently, in evaluating employees, most Phase One firms ignore international experience or, worse yet, treat it as hindering potential career advancement.

6.4.2 Phase Two

Unlike Phase One's domestic focus, Phase Two firms are multidomestic or polycentric. They respond to competition by expanding from domestic to international operations, including actively marketing internationally and beginning to assemble and to produce abroad. They are differentiated into distinct national markets and operations, and only minimally integrated regionally or firmwide.

For Phase Two firms, we would predict that the international staff would primarily be functionaries. Home country marketing representatives are frequently selected and sent to sell products in specific foreign countries. Technical experts are sent to transfer technology to specific foreign production sites, and similarly, managing directors and financial officers are assigned abroad to control overall country operations. Since most R&D, and thus most innovation, still takes place in the firm's home country, firms generally view foreign operations primarily as sites for replicating that which has already been done at home.

Both the Phase One and the Phase Two approaches would be inconceivable if international activities were considered central to the firm's operations and success. While international assignment are more numerous than in Phase One, Phase Two's international managers[4] still experience lower status and influence than their home country counterparts.

6.4.2.1 Criteria for Phase Two IHRM

Unlike the previous phase, cross-cultural sensitivity and foreign language skills become extremely important for the Phase Two international manager's effectiveness. Given the competition, firms can create a comparative advantage by producing culturally appropriate products, using culturally appropriate management techniques, and marketing in culturally appropriate ways. To effectively implement these culturally appropriate strategies, international managers themselves need to develop cross-cultural skills.[5]

Unfortunately however, while numerous techniques exist, American firms generally have not recognized the importance of cross-cultural training to international effectiveness for the Phase Two organization. Schwind (1985) claims that "a majority of companies involved in international trade do not provide any preparatory training for managers and employees destined to work abroad". Consistent with Schwind's observation, Mendenhall and Oddou (1986: 77) note that "there is a marked

---

[4] For a discussion of Phase Two selection practices see, among others, Baker & Ivancevich (1971); Miller (1973); Hawes & Kealy (1981); Tung (1981); Church (1982); Torbiorn (1982); Abe & Wiseman (1983); Oddou & Mendenhall (1984); Mendenhall & Oddou (1985); and Zeira & Banai (1985).

[5] For a discussion of cross-cultural training approaches and techniques, see among others, Hall (1959); Oberg (1960); Smalley (1963); Byrnes (1966); Guthrie (1967); Higbee (1969); Torbiorn (1982); Oddou & Mendenhall (1984) and Mendenhall & Oddou (1985).

deficiency on the part of U.S. firms in offering comprehensive cross-cultural training to their employees who are assigned overseas". Tung (1981) corroborates others' observations with empirical evidence[6], reporting in 1982 that only 32% of U.S. companies conducted formal international training programs, as compared with 57% of Japanese companies and 69% of European companies. Ronen (1986) has noted that the 32% reported in Tung's 1982 study is the same figure as reported in earlier research by Baker and Ivancevich (1971): "this figure has remained virtually unchanged over the last two decades even though large numbers of overseas managers have indicated that proper pre-departure preparation is absolutely necessary to improve overseas performance" (Ronen, 1986: 548). This low and unchanging level of expatriate training in U.S. companies again exposes Phase One assumptions ill-fitted to the Phase Two, Three and Four environments.

Moreover, this low and unchanging level of training also provides one explanation for America's high expatriate failure rates, 25 to 49% (Mendenhall & Oddou, 1985), when compared with Europe's and Japan's (see Tung, 1982). What it does not explain is the acceptance of such high rates, especially when Tung (1982) has found a correlation of −.63 between expatriate failure rates and the rigor of the selection and training procedure used. Once again, the problem appears to be that firms operating in a Phase Two environment continue to make Phase One assumptions as an unquestioned convenience in their human resource planning.

Phase Two firms generally evaluate expatriate performance based on that of the foreign operation. Yet, even the best evaluations rarely lead to significant career advancement. Most returnees from foreign assignments find re-entry extremely difficult. While abroad, the firm frequently views them as out-of-sight and out-of-mind. As returnees, it sees them as out-of-date and unimportant. To returnees' disappointment, their colleagues often evaluate them as somewhat inconsequential to the domestic mainstream (see Schein's [1971] discussion linking centrality in the organization to career advancement). For ambitious managers who want to make it to the top of Phase Two firms, going abroad is generally a bad career strategy. (For a discussion of reentry, see, among others, Howard, 1973; Adler, 1981, 1991; and Harvey, 1982.)

---

[6] For similar observations, see Korn/Ferry International (1981); Runzheimer (1984); Dunbar & Ehrlich (1986); and Mendenhall, Dunbar, and Oddou (1986).

Similarly, host nationals rarely, if ever, become senior executives in Phase Two firms. In most cases, an invisible ceiling stops them at the level of the country managing director. To get beyond this invisible ceiling, one must hold a passport from the firm's home country. The almost complete absence, until very recently, of non-Americans on the boards of directors of American firms (and the similar scarcity of non-Japanese on Japanese boards) underscores the strength of the invisible ceiling.

6.4.3 Phase Three

By Phase Three, the competitive environment again changes. Price, rather than either product or market, allows Phase Three firms to ssucceed in the now worldwide markets. Geographical dispersion often increases and with it the firm's need to integrate. This geographical dispersion not only includes divisions within the firm, but also worldwide supplier, manufacturer, and distributor networks external to the firm. Phase Three firms accomplish integration primarily through centralizing and standardizing as many aspects of their products, processes, and structure as possible.

6.4.3.1 Criteria for Phase Three IHRM

Given the critical role that multinational production and operations play in corporate survival, successful Phase Three firms select their best, rather than their marginal, employees for international positions. Managers assigned to international positions ideally come from throughout the worldwide organization, rather than just from the home country.

One of the explicit purposes of international assignments, beyond getting-the-job-done, becomes firmwide integration. The firm uses international positions to develop an integrated, global organization through the international career development of high potential managers and thus the creation of a global cadre of executives. Similar to the role global lines of business play in integrating Phase Three products and markets worldwide, the international cadre of executives takes on a central role of integrating the firm through its top managers.[7]

---

[7] See Edstrom and Galbraith (1977) for a discussion of the use of international transfers as an organizational development strategy.

Whereas Phase Three makes international experience essential to firm-wide management and career advancement, the importance of cross-cultural sensitivity and language skills diminishes somewhat. Rather than using cultural diversity, Phase Three firms often either assume or create similarity when attempting to integrate the global firm. For example, they frequently assume that consumers' tastes are essentially similar worldwide, thus allowing the firm to create generic products and services and to benefit from substantial economies of scope and scale (see Leavitt, 1983, for an excellent exposition of this position).

Moreover, organization culture is assumed to dominate national culture. Under the rubric of organization culture, firms generally require foreign nationals to accommodate to the parent company's, and implicitly the parent culture's, styles of interacting. The underlying assumption is that cultural differences either can be ignored because the organization culture has molded nationals of all countries into similar employees, professionals who are "beyond passport", or must be minimized because such differences cause problems (see Adler, 1983). The first assumption becomes apparent in the lack of recognition for varying cultural styles of conducting business; that is, in the firm's cultural-blindness. The second assumption becomes apparent in such behaviors as the decision to use English exclusively, or the selection of host nationals who exhibit attitudes and behaviors most typical of the parent company's culture. Many North American companies traditionally have recruited host nationals from U.S. and Canadian college campuses to insure that new hires would have an excellent command of English and an adequate socialization into North American ways of doing business. In this way, North American firms have been able to hire North Americanized foreigners, rather than candidates more typical of their home country and culture.

In summary, Phase Three differs fundamentally from prior phases in that the primary location of cross-cultural interaction moves inside the organization. Phase One firms encountered little cross-cultural interaction because both their employees and their clients are from the same domestic environment. Phase Two firms encounter cultural differences when interacting with their external environment, primarily as home company nationals attempt to market abroad and to manage foreign workers. By contrast, Phase Three firms, having hired people from around the world and integrated them into the overall organization, encounter cultural differences within the firm's internal organizational culture. The human resource management systems should reflect the location of the cultural diversity. Unfortunately however, as has been described, Phase three firms often attempt to assume away the cultural differences by choosing to believe that organizational culture overrides differences in national perspective and behavior. Research, however, has shown this assumption of similarity to be incorrect. Organizational culture neither dominates nor erases national culture, but rather, in the case of multinational corporations, appears to accentuate it.[8]

Re-entry in this environment poses less of a problem than in prior phases. Because firms value international experience, they often select top people to send abroad, recognize their international accomplishments, and bring them back to significant positions. Rather than hurting the expatriate's career, international assignments often become essential for career success.

6.4.4 Phase Four

In Phase Four, which combines aspects of Phases One, Two, and Three, firms face severe competition on a global scale. Successful strategies involve producing least-cost, top-quality products that, while differentiated for individual tastes, are produced globally and marketed globally. The increased severity of global competition forces multinationals to re-examine their traditional (Phase One, Two, and Three) approaches to human resource management (see Pucik, 1984).

6.4.4.1 Criteria for Phase Four IHRM

The Phase Four environment requires firms to assign their best people to international positions, because, by this time, the overwhelming dominance of the domestic market has receded to a relic of the past. Key employees must be multilingual and culturally sensitive to identify the needs of culturally differentiated market segments and to respond quickly and appropriately to each. Moreover, top-quality, least-cost production necessitates worldwide operations, with location dictated by strategic, political, and economic constraints, along with the supply of inputs and market access. Hence, people from all over the world constantly must communicate and

---

[8] See Hofstede (1980) for a study of the cultural diversity within IBM's corporate culture and Laurent (1983) for a study of cultural differences within a number of major American and European corporations, and Adler (1991) for a summary of both.

work with each other: in the vernacular, they must "think globally and act locally" to become managers (see Murray and Murray, 1986). Boundaries between expatriate and local personnel become obsolete (Doz and Prahalad, 1986). Neither cultural forms of control emphasizing more homogeneous selection, socialization and training nor more bureaucratic forms of control can independently address the needs for integration and differentiation (see Jaeger, 1983; and Baliga and Jaeger, 1984). The first emphasizes integration through eliminating differences while the second emphasizes integration by controlling differences. The former is more appropriate to Phase Three's highly centralized organization while the later fits best with Phase Two's emphasis on decentralization. Because neither simultaneously emphasize integration and differentiation, neither fits particularly well in Phase Four.

Effectively managing such a culturally diverse organizational culture becomes an essential Phase Four skill. As Doz and Prahalad (1986) note, multinational corporations must find new ways to manage the dichotomy of cultural diversity and global integration, of national responsiveness and centralized coordination and control. One of the firm's major competitive weapons is its ability to use global human resources along both dimensions, to enhance national responsiveness and global integration.

6.4.4.2 Problems

By Phase Four, cross-cultural interaction takes place both within the firm and between the firm and its external environment. Consequently, understanding and managing cultural differences becomes essential both internally and externally. The firm's home country culture can no longer dominate its organization culture. Ignoring or minimizing cultural diversity has become a luxury of the past, as the firm must now continually recognize and manage it. In no case can the firm ignore the differences (see Adler, 1983; Adler and Bartholomew, 1992a and 1992b; Adler and Graham, 1989).

Cultural diversity, by increasing differentiation, makes integration more difficult. However, if managed appropriately, cultural differences become a key Phase Four resource. For example, when they need differentiation firms that recognize cultural diversity can use the differences to gain multiple perspectives, develop wider ranges of options and approaches, heighten creativity and problem solving skills, and thereby increase flexibility in addressing culturally distinct client and colleague systems. Simultaneously however, these same firms must be able to create similarity from the diversity when they need integration. This consciously created universality, Phase Four's form of organizational culture, uses cultural differences to heighten coordination and control.[9] Unlike firms in the prior phases, global Phase Four firms never assume similarity nor rely on naturally occurring universality to heighten integration: they create similarity, they create – "universals".

Re-entry problems diminish significantly given the centrality of global operations and the need for highly trained, experienced, and sophisticated managers. Because of this global perspective, international human resource management is no longer marginal, but becomes central to firmwide success. Without a human resource system well integrated into the firm's global strategy, the Phase Four firm will not succeed. With anything other than a global perspective, the human resource system will cause the Phase Four firm to fail.

6.5   Future Research Implications

Some of the research ideas presented in this section were developed in the discussions at the conference on Research for Relevance. They were in response to the framework presented in Adler's opening address, as summarized in the preceding sections.

6.5.1   Importance of Product and Business Phase

The most salient research issue which emerges is the need to conduct studies of strategic HRM effectiveness within the contextual framework which specifically addresses the phase of business development. The framework predicts the types of cross-cultural skills and training needed for each stage of internationalization.

Phase One firms are most effective if they focus on domestic operations. In Phase Two, internationally posted managers must be culturally sensitive to and able to interact with particular local markets. In Phase Three, the skills of cultural integration become paramount, both for internationally posted managers as well as for those who are domestically

---

[9] For a discussion of cultural synergy, see Adler (1991 Chapter 4).

based. This assumes a certain degree of international experience as well as a firm grounding in the home corporate culture.

6.5.2 Increasing Importance of Phase Four

Many of today's firms now face a global economy. "Fully 70% ... [of U.S.A.] industries, up from 25% only a dozen years ago, are under full-scale attack by foreign competitors" (Peters, 1984: 11). Some firms have changed, while many will have to change significantly to compete successfully in the 1990's and the twenty-first century. Unfortunately, whereas most other functional areas of the firm have already begun to respond, many firms' human resources systems have failed to adapt sufficiently to this changing environment. In all too many cases, human resource systems are managed as if they were in Phase One, Two, or Three, not in the global world that is nor in the multi-phase world that will be. In one particularly astute indictment, Kobrin (1988) challenged the fundamental premise on which American firms base their overall human resource management policies and their specific expatriate decisions:

> Both managers and academics note a number of good business reasons for the replacement of expatriates by local nationals including environmental competence and cost reduction. ... I dissent ... Although all of the reasons given for the phasing out of expatriates are valid, I suggest that one that is not discussed actually dominates: The difficulty many Americans have had adapting to overseas assignments and the abysmally high failure rates they have experienced. Put simply, Americans have not been able to handle working and living in other cultures and U.S. MNC's have found it easier to replace them with foreign nationals than to make an effort to solve the underlying problem (Kobrin, 1988: 1).

Clearly the need for research on the requirements and training of successful managers in Phase Four organizations is critical. Similarly, identifying the typical problems encountered by these firms in managing the culturally diverse workforce is an important research agenda. Some of the problems stem from the inability of the HR area to keep pace with the firm's business strategy transition from Phase One, Two, and Three into Phase Four. Thus, a yet unproven research question is whether the high level of cross-cultural sensitivity and managerial skills needed in this phase can be appropriately identified and developed (see Adler and Bartholomew, 1992a and 1992b). Similarly, management scholars will need to use multiple levels of analysis when studying international HRM of the

Phase Four organization: the industry, the firm, the subunit, the group and the individual (see Boyacigiller and Adler, 1992).

6.5.3 Domestic Global Management

An important issue which transcends that of the phase model is domestic globalization. In the late 1950's and 1960's a dichotomous view of the world prevailed; there was a tendency to view things as domestic versus foreign. Research, for example, tended to consider market penetration as occurring in either a domestic or foreign context. However in the mid-1970's, a new phenomenon emerged, the globalization of the domestic market. With the filtering of globalization into the home territory, there was really no longer any such thing as a purely domestic market. To keep pace with the reality of domestic multiculturalism and "domestic" international marketing, research must now shift its focus to globalization "over here" rather than just "over there".

For Americans, the continued interest in domestic versus international markets could be a product of past United States stability and experience. European companies, even domestic ones, have always had to be more cognizant of a global or regional economy than have most American firms. Similarly, Canadian firms have never been able to afford to overlook the market to the south of them or the impact of the "foreign investment" imposed on them. With the filtering of globalization into the U.S. home territory, it has become more evident that even prior to 1970 there had never been such a phenomenon as a purely domestic market.

6.5.4 Domestic Global Human Resources Management

One research topic of immediate interest may be an assessment of the impact of globalization on domestic markets and the consequences which this has for human resource. Managers in domestically focused firms will need to "go international" in order to survive as the environment of local, domestic firms becomes globalized and subject to daily international influences. For example, U.S.-based firms selling only to their local market need to understand their foreign-based competitors' production, marketing and HRM strategies. The establishment of Mazda, Honda, and Toyota plants in North America are examples of such international competition in the automotive industry. The key question is which domestic firms will be thinking proactively and preparing their HR systems accordingly, rather than remaining reactive and attempting to compete while domestically disadvantaged.

The size of a firm may be an important variable on the proactive-reactive dimension. Larger firms with greater international exposure may tend to be forced earlier to assume a more internationally proactive stance. Smaller, purely domestic firms may remain internationally reactive because of a lack of awareness. Another variable may be the extent of the tradition of competing domestically with foreign-based firms. Canada, to a much greater extent than the U.S., has always had to be highly conscious of competition with its southern neighbor on its home territory. A Canadian response to domestic globalization has been the establishment of joint ventures between domestic firms and their foreign-based competitors. The joint venture between GM and Suzuki, and other joint ventures with Japanese firms in Canada, illustrate of this strategy.

6.5.5 Illusion of Domestic Management

In even the most proactive firms, however, there may remain the illusion of domestic management.[10] As Adler pointed out, international managers are aware of having to "turn on" their international skills when working abroad with foreign clients, but when they come home to their own organizational culture, they often act as if they can set these skills aside. The assumption is that, at home, home rules operate no matter how "international" the context. There is a lack of realization that the home rules are being changed by the presence of foreign competition in the home country; a most notable example is the influence of the Japanese culture on work norms in North America.

Thus, when the Japanese set up plants in North America, they will not do business with factories that are not spotlessly clean. Most North American firms have never cared whether their factories were spotless or not. Domestic firms, in order to conduct business, must realize that change in the competitive environment is not in their hands. This change, of course,

---

[10] See Adler and Bartholomew (1992b) for a discussion of domestic illusions.

is not confined to the United States. All economies, including the Japanese, are now dictated by international rules. From a research perspective, it is essential that academics also realize that the rules are changing and redirect their attentions appropriately, most notably to take into consideration the cultural context and the global environment (see Boyacigiller and Adler, 1991 and 1992; Adler and Bartholomew, 1992a and b).

6.6 Conclusion

Important research issues are suggested by the Four Phase model; more importantly, it produces a framework for analyzing IHRM needs, for assessing the potential success of international assignments, and for resolving problems resulting from a firm's mismatch of its international human resource system with the cultural requirements of gobal business competition. The research agenda is clear. Management scholars need to study human resource management in context. To study HRM out of context is not only no longer helpful, it is misleading.

6.7 References

Abe, H. & R.L. Wiseman (1983). A Cross Cultural Confirmation of the Dimension of Intercultural Effectiveness. *International Journal of Intercultural Relations,* 7(1), 53–68.

Adler, N.J. (1981). Re-entry: Managing Cross-Cultural Transitions. *Group and Organization Studies,* 6(3), 341–356.

Adler, N.J. (1983). Organizational Development in a Multicultural Environment. *Journal of Applied Behavioral Science,* 11(3), 349–365.

Adler, N.J. (1991). *International Dimensions of Organizational Behavior. 2nd ed.* Boston: PWS-Kent Publishing.

Adler, N.J. and S. Bartholomew (1992a). Academic and Professional Communities of Discourse: Generating Knowledge on Transnational Human Resource Management. *Journal of International Business Studies* (in press).

Adler, N.J. and S. Bartholomew (1992b). Managing Globally competent people. *Academy of Management Executive* (in press).

Adler, N.J. and J.L. Graham. (1989). Cross-cultural Interaction: The International Comparison Fallacy. *Journal of International Business Studies,* 20(3), 513–537.

Adler N.J. and M. Jelinek (1986). Is 'Organization Culture' Culture Bound? *Human Resource Management,* 25(1), 73–90.

Baker, J.C. and J.M. Ivancevich (1971). The Assignment of American Executives Abroad: Systematic, Haphazards, or Chaotic? *California Management Review,* 13(3), 33–44.

Baliga, B.R. & A.M. Jaeger (1984). Multinational Corporations: Control Systems and Delegation Issues. *Journal of International Business Studies,* 15(2), 25–40.

Bartlett, C.A. and S. Ghoshal (1989). *Managing Across Borders: The Transnational Solution.* Boston, MA: Harvard Business School Press.

Boyacigiller, N. and N.J. Adler (1991). The Parochial Dinosaur: The Organizational Sciences in a Global Context. *Academy of Management Review,* 16(2), 262–290.

Boyacigiller, N. and N.J. Adler (1992). Insiders and Outsiders: Bridging the Worlds of Organizational Behavior and International Management. Presented at the Perspectives on International Business: Theory, Research, and International Arrangements Conference, University of South Carolina, May.

Byrnes, F.C. (1966). Role Shock: An Occupational Hazard of American Technical Assistants Abroad. *The Annals,* 368, 95–108.

Church, A. T. (1982). Sojourner Adjustment. *Psychology Bulletin,* 91(3), 540–571.

Davis, S. (1987). *Future Prefect.* Redding Mass.: Addison-Wesley.

Doz, Y.L. and C.K. Prahalad (1986). Controlled variety: A challenge for human resource management in the MNC. *Human Resource Management,* 25(1), 55–72.

Dunbar, E. and M. Ehrlich (1986). *International Human Resource Practices, Selecting, Training, and Managing the International Staff: A Survey Report.* The Project on International Human Resources. New York: Columbia University Teachers College.

Edstrom, A. and J.R. Galbraith (1977). Transfer of Managers as a Coordination and Control Strategy in Multinational Organizations. *Administrative Science Quarterly,* 22(2), 248–268.

Galbraith, J.R. and R.K Kazanjian (1986). Organizing to Implement: Sategies of Diversity and Globalization: The Role of Matrix Design. *Human Resource Management* 25(1), 37–54.

Ghadar, F. (1977). *The Evolution of OPEC Strategy.* Lexington, Mass.: Lexington Books.

Ghadar, F. (1985). Political Risk and the Erosion of Control: The Case of the Oil Industry. In T. Brewer (ed.), *Political Risks in International*

Business: New Dimensions for Research Management, and Public Policy. New York: Praeger, 59–70.

Ghadar, F. (1986). Strategic Considerations in the Financing of International Investment. In P. Grub, F. Ghadar, and D. Khambata (eds.), *The Multinational Enterprise in Transition,* Revised edition. Princeton, N.J.: The Darwin Press.

Guthrie, G.M. (1967). Cultural Preparation for the Philippines. In R.B. Textor (ed.), *Cultural Frontiers of the Peace Corps.* Cambridge, Mass: MIT Press.

Hall, E.T. (1959). *The Silent Language.* New York: Doubleday.

Harvey, M.G. (1982). The Other side of Foreign Assignments: Dealing with the Repatriation Dilemma. *Columbia Journal of World Business,* 17(1), 53–59.

Hawes, F. and D.J. Kealey (1981). An Empirical Study of Canadian Technical Assistance. *International Journal of Intercultural Relations,* 5(3), 239–258.

Hedlund, G. (1986). The Hypermodern MNC-a Heterarchy?. *Human Resource Management,* 25(1), 9–36.

Higbee, H. (1969). Role Shock-a New Concept. *International Educational and Cultural Exchange,* 4(4), 71–81.

Hofstede, G. (1980). *Culture's Consequences: International Differences In Work-Related Values.* Beverly Hills, CA: Sage.

Howard, C. G. (1973). The Expatriate Manager and the Role of the MNC. *Personnel Journal,* 48(1), 25–29.

Jaeger, A.M. (1983). The Transfer of Organizational Culture Overseas: An Approach to Control in the Multinational Corporation. *Journal of International Business Studies,* 14(2), 91–114.

Kobrin, S.J. (1988). Expatiate Reduction and Strategic Control in American Multinational Organizational Corporations, *Human Resource Management,* 27, 16–29.

Korn-Ferry International (1981). *A Study of the Repatriation of the American International Executive.* New York: Korn-Ferry.

Laurent, A. (1983). The Cultural Diversity of Western Management Conceptions. *International Studies of Management and Organization.* 8(1–2), 75–96.

Laurent, A. (1986). The Cross-cultural Puzzle of International Human Resource Management, *Human Resources Management,* 25(1), 91–102.

Leavitt, T. (1983). The Globalization of Markets. *Harvard Business Review,* 61(3), 92–102.

Lorange, P. (1986). Human resource management in multinational cooperative ventures. *Human Resource Management,* 25(1), 91–102.

Mendenhall, M.E., E. Dunbar, and G.R. Oddou (1986). The State of the
Art of Overseas Relocation Programs in U.S. Multinationals. Presented
at the Academy of International Business Annual Meetings, London,
November.

Mendenhall, M.E. and G.R. Oddou (1985). The dimensions of expatriate
acculturation: A Review. *Academy of Management Review,* 10(1), 39–
47.

Mendenhall, M.E. and G.R. Oddou (1986). Acculturation Profiles of Expatriate Managers: Implications for Cross-cultural Training Programs.
Columbia Journal of World Business, 21(4), 73–79.

Miller, E. L. (1973). The international selection decision: A study of some
dimensions of managerial behavior in the selection decision process.
Academy of Management Journal, 16(2), 239–252.

Miller, E.L, S.Beechler, B. Bhatt and R. Nath (1986). The Relationship
Between the Global Strategic Planning Process and the Human Resource Management Function. *Human Resource Planning,* 9(1), 9–23.

Murray, F.T. and A.H. Murray (1986). Global Managers for Global Businesses. *Sloan Management Review,* 27(2), 75–80.

Oberg, K. (1960). Culture Shock: Adjustment to New Cultural Environments. *Practical Anthropology,* 7, 177–182.

Oddou, G. and M. Mendenhall (1984). Person perception in cross-cultural
settings: A review of Cross-cultural and Related Literature. *International Journal of Intercultural Relations,* 8(1), 77–96.

Peters, T. (1984). Competition and Compassion. *California Management
Review,* 26(4), 11–26.

Pucik, V. (1984). The International Management of Human Resources. In
C. Fombrun, N. Tichy and M.A. Devanna (eds.), *Strategic Human Resource Management.* New York: John Wiley and Sons, 403–419.

Ronen, S.(1986). *Comparative and Multinational Management.* New York:
John Wiley.

Runzheimer Executive Report. (1984). *1984 Expatriation/Repatriation
Survey. Number 31.* Rochester WI: Runzheimer, 1–38.

Schein, E.H. (1971). The Individual, the Organization, and the Career: A
Conceptual Scheme. *Journal of Applied Behavioral Science,* 7(4), 401–
426.

Schwind, H. (1985). The State of the Art in Cross-cultural management
Training, In R. Doctor (ed.) *International Human Resource Development Annual,* 1, 7–15.

Smalley, W. A. (1963). Culture Shock, Language Shock, and the Shock of Self-Discovery. *Practical Anthropology,* 10, 49–56.

Torbiorn, I. (1982). *Living Abroad: Personal Adjustment and Personnel Policy in Overseas Settings.* New York: John Wiley and Sons.

Tung, R. (1981). Selection and Training of Personnel for Overseas Assignments. *Columbia Journal of World Business,* 16(1), 57–71.

Tung, R. (1982). Selection and Training Procedures of U. S., European and Japanese Multinationals. *California Management Review,* 25(1), 57–71.

Tung, R. (1984). *Key to Japan's Economic Success: Human Power.* Lexington, MA: Lexington Books.

Vernon, R. (1966). International Investment and International Trade in the Product Cycle. *Quarterly Journal of Economics,* 80(2), 190–207.

Vernon, R. (1971). *Sovereignty at Bay: The Multinational Spread of U.S. Enterprises.* New York: Basic Books.

Vernon, R. (1981). Sovereignty at Bay Ten Years After. *International Organization,* 25(5), 517–529.

Zeira, Y. and M. Banai (1985). Selection of Expatriate Managers in MNCs: The Host-environment Point of View. *International Studies of Management and Organization,* 15(1), 33–5.

7 Beyond Bureaucracy: Towards a Comparative Analysis of Forms of Economic Resource Coordination and Control

S. Gordon Redding
University of Hong Kong

7.1 Introduction

The post-war economic success of Japanese and other Asian enterprises has stimulated considerable interest in their forms of organization and the relations they have with the wider society. Together with a growing awareness of variations in European business structures, and the historical specificity of the United States' experience (Chandler, 1981; Locke, 1984), this success has emphasized the contextual nature of economic organization and the limited utility of general management prescriptions drawn from a single culture. In particular the generalization of rational-legal authority principles and formal bureaucratic control systems as the only efficient way of coordinating and directing economic resources in competitive markets seems less valid than it did to Max Weber and their efficacy much more dependent on extra-economic institutions than most management textbook authors have recognized. The more recent growth of the "four little dragons", South Korea, Taiwan, Hong Kong and Singapore, has in addition drawn attention to the limitations of Anglo-saxon conceptions of legally bounded firms as the basic unit of economic action. In both the chaebol and the overseas Chinese family business it is quite clear that the formal legal cum financial unit is not the critical decision making entity and extra-firm linkages are critical to an understanding of economic actions (Jones and Sakong, 1980; Redding and Tam, 1985). Furthermore, these linkages are often not only contractual or bureaucratic, as Williamson (1975) proposed in his opposition of markets and hierarchies, but are also highly personal and family dependent. Just as cartelization and interlocking shareholdings amongst members of industrial groups can be considered viable alternative means of coordinating economic actors' activities (cf. Bauer and Cohen, 1981; Daems, 1983) to the diversified multi-divisional enterprise, so too kinship based trust relationships appear effective ways of integrating diverse activities in Chinese family businesses.

These points suggest that the traditional concern with independent legal entities which are well bounded and distinct from their environments needs to be modified and the institutionalization of such atomistic firms as the dominant form of economic actor needs to be seen as a contingent historical phenomenon which is by no means essential to economic development. Furthermore, it now seems clear that different forms of economic resource coordination and control can be equally successful in world markets and this success can only be adequately understood in terms of the broader social context in which they develop and become institutionalized. Theories of economic activity and change which treat dominant economic actors as discrete, homogeneous entities pursuing identical "rationalities" need, then, to be replaced by approaches that consider their form and operation as contingent, socially contextual phenomena varying across cultures and historical periods.

In proposing a comparative analysis of forms of economic coordination and control in this paper we wish to emphasize the need to go beyond previous discussions of organizations and their "environments" that presume the unproblematic nature of boundaries and identity of economic actors and examine how particular kinds of coordination and control systems develop and are institutionalized in particular societies. Rather than just "breaking down" the organization, as Callon and Vignolle (1977) have suggested, we propose to consider the different processes by which different sorts of economic actors are "built up" in distinct socio-cultural contexts and are able to compete internationally in world markets. Essentially, the questions to be addressed are: how do different forms of economic organization become established in different societies, how do they coordinate and control different sorts of human and material resources and how do they manage extra-enterprise connections and develop distinctive strategies in different social contexts?

As a preliminary step in dealing with these general questions we will outline the sorts of considerations which we think are critical to a comparative analysis of economic activities and briefly describe how these are manifested in the case of overseas Chinese family business, with passing reference also to the Korean *chaebol* and the Japanese *zaibatsu*. Initially we consider the problem of identifying the appropriate unit of analysis for comparing economic actors and then propose a set of dimensions for describing and contrasting organizational configurations before considering their application to these cases.

This approach directly impacts the issue of relevance that is the theme of this volume by raising again the question of what organizational structures are most significant to international management research, that is, what is the relevant unit of analysis. Although many of this volume's contributors explicitly recognized the importance of understanding the impact of the cultural, social and economic factors on the firm (see for example, Peterson [Chapter 3] and Adler and Ghadar [Chapter 6], they have defined the relevant unit of analysis to be the MNC. For Adler and Ghadar, strategic decisions are made by the MNC management in response to evolving environmental and product-market forces. For Rugman [see Chapter 9] too, the relevant unit of analysis remains the MNC but the field of inquiry widens to include the interaction of the firm and government and regulatory bodies. In broadening the relevant unit of analysis here to include those institution, personal and familial extra firm linkages that coordinate economic activity in the Japanese, Korean firms and in the Chinese family business, we hope to identify in Mintzberg's terms (Chapter 8) "truly different types global firms" and move beyond the global ethnocentricity that confines us to the study of the rationalized Western model MNC.

The description of these radically different forms is also consistent with Peterson's (Chapter 3) call to tease out the impact of cultural, political, and socio-economic theories on performance. Indeed, Miller (Chapter 10) sees the field becoming more relevant if it can view the corporation as a laboratory for testing new organizational models. The Asian models that will be discussed here are becoming less novel to the West every year. The zaibatsu, kaisha and chaebol are already becoming better known even as Western economies become defensive over their success. A greater understanding of these forms, as well as the Chinese family business, will become even more relevant to both researcher and practitioner as trade and cooperation between East and West continues to grow.

7.2 The Unit of Economic Action

In comparing economic actors and explaining why they vary across human societies it is clearly critical to be able to identify the same unit of analysis in different contexts. Equally clearly, the way in which this is done will substantially affect any subsequent analysis since what is "inside" or "outside" organizational boundaries in different societies, and so an important feature of forms of economic organization, will have already been determined. In dealing with this difficulty, and others, it is important to bear in mind the theoretical purpose of the analysis which here is the comparison of forms of economic resource coordination and control. The unit of analysis, then, is that entity which acquires, allocates, directs and sells economic resources in a relatively cohesive and reproducible manner in order to generate products or services traded in some market system.

As Penrose (1959) suggests, "firms" in this sense are administrative structures which select and combine human and material resources and manage their transformation into productive service in a coherent and coordinated way. Economic actors are, then, relatively autonomous entities which organize resources in particular ways and reproduce themselves as distinct social systems making economic decisions. Their key features can be summarized as:

1. a relative autonomy as resource acquirer, disposer and controller;
2. some reproduced administrative system which is minimally stable; and
3. a relatively integrated and coordinated information and strategic decision making system.

This system is responsible for business entry and exit decisions, product and market changes, major technical investments, senior management appointments and rewards and overall financial policies. In considering, for example, whether Japanese *zaibatsu* and French industrial groups or their constituent firms should be considered the dominant economic actors, the critical questions are: which entity controls senior personnel selections decision, decides retention ratios and allocation of profits, makes major investment decisions and market changes, and becomes the dominant unit of loyalty and identity for senior managerial personnel. In practice, of course, it is rarely possible to identify unequivocally the locus of these sorts of decisions but it is usually feasible to make considered judgements about the dominant economic entity on the basis of case studies and general economic histories. It seems clear, for instance, that the once dominant position of the general trading company *zaibatsu* in the Japanese economy has declined in the past 20 or so years and newer *kaisha* which group subcontractors around a dominant manufacturing concern have become significant economic actors (Abegglen and Stalk, 1987). In analyzing contemporary Japanese enterprises, then, both types of economic actor have to be considered and the processes by which the once dominant form has changed, spelled out.

Having identified, however tentatively, the dominant forms of economic coordination and control in different societies the next task is to identify the major dimensions on which they vary and develop so that the significant differences between them can be understood in terms of their contexts. In addition to the traditional means of distinguishing formal organization structures, such as those developed for comparing "western" managerial bureaucracies, these need to include broader characteristics such as the relations between economic institutions and other major social institutions, especially kinship groupings and state agencies (Hamilton and Biggart, 1988), and general principles of authority and loyalty. They also have to incorporate processes of inter-enterprise coordination and cooperation as well as variations in the scope of economic activities undertaken and in the institutionalization of enterprise boundaries. These dimensions summarize differences in particular "recipes" for organizing economic actors which have been established in different societies and seem to work relatively effectively in them These recipes structure constituent elements in different ways and are derived from particular features of their society contexts. We now turn to a consideration of how these recipes can be differentiated and the major characteristics of social formations which lead to different sorts of economic organization becoming dominant in different societies.

7.3 Forms of Economic Organization and their Contents

A preliminary listing of the constituent elements of economic recipes institutionalized in different contexts would include such features as the nature of the people who establish economic actors, how they control and direct resources, the sorts of resources combined, the characteristic markets served, and the mechanisms of linkage to other actors such as suppliers, customers, competitors and the state. Other aspects include the scope and size of activities typically undertaken, the growth strategies followed and the decision-making systems used.

This rather ad hoc and in principle limitless list can be reduced and rendered more useful by drawing simple distinctions between those features which are primarily characteristic of the internal systems of resource acquisition, coordination and control, those which are primarily characteristic of relations between economic actors and other major actors, and those which characterize distinctive aspects of the societal contexts in which different sorts of economic actor become established. While these distinctions are undoubtedly too simple to deal with the complex interdependencies of social phenomena and process, they serve to structure the analysis and provide an initial means of organizing the argument.

Turning first to the societal contexts which structure the sorts of economic organization that become established, various authors have emphasized the critical role of dominant cultural values in explaining variations between enterprise systems and, in particular, the significance of "post-Confucian" ethics and social norms in the growth of east Asian economies since the War (Kahn, 1979; Hofheinz and Calder, 1982). The sorts of values and ethical precepts which have been adumbrated in these analyses include such general preferences as a work ethic, consensus rather than open conflict, the primacy of personal and family relationships, perceptions of "power distance" and acceptance of hierarchical relations and so on. Typically these have been rather ad hoc and used to explain specific features of enterprise organization manifested in particular societies or else inferred from survey data through statistical manipulation.

The obvious importance of general cultural preferences in organizing social relationship and of social conventions about appropriate patterns of behaviour and conceptions of personal identity for coordination and control processes in economic enterprises need not imply cultural determinism or the ontological primacy of patterns of value orientation in the constitution of social phenomena. As social constructions, though, economic organizations are clearly constrained by the dominant system of ordering social relations in a society and the social order within such organizations is substantially constituted by the broad value orientations of participants which set appropriate standards of behaviour, define individual and group identities and establish the bases of social interactions. One of the most systematic approaches to the analysis of value orientations in social systems is, of course, that of Talcott Parsons (1951) and it is intuitively easy to see how his set of five "pattern variables" can be used to distinguish between the successful east Asian societies as well as western ones and how they are manifested in different forms of economic organization and control. We shall briefly discuss their application to the expatriate Chinese family business later in this chapter. These basic patterns of value orientation are strongly connected to the dominant principles of legitimating authority and hierarchical relations within societies which in turn structure authority relations within enterprises. Authority principles are also associated with bases of solidarity within and between organizations in that where loyalty to vertical hierarchies dominates loyalty to specialized, externally certified expertise, commitment to large managerial bureaucracies is likely to be greater than where notions of "professional" skills and identity are strongly institutionalized and serve to fragment organizational identities as in the U.S.A. and the U.K.. This loyalty to vertical hierarchies in turn reflects historical patterns of social integration which provide a continuing chain of loyalties from peasants to the apex of national authority such as in some forms of feudalism. Societies which do not have such a continuous systems of integrating loyalties vertically are unlikely to develop stable large coordination and control systems which systematically integrate diverse economic activities because the general social basis of commitment to large collective entities does not exist.

This point is related to the general phenomenon, discussed by Durkheim and many writers on modernization, of institutional pluralism and the growth of supra family organizations which are able to mobilize loyalties. Typically, the development of some institutional differentiation and of mediating organizations between kinship units and sovereign power units has been seen as crucial to the formation of separate economic enterprises controlling resources and competing on a market basis. The examples of industrialization in East Asian societies suggest this view needs some modification, at least in its simplest and strongest form, but clearly the development of relatively autonomous, privately controlled, units of resource coordination requires the existence of institutions which permit the private acquisition of resources and legitimize the private disposition and use of them. In order for large economic organizations controlling substantial resources on a societal wide scale to become established, dominant groups, and especially the sovereign institution, must accept some diffusion and pluralism of resource control and, equally, plural sources of loyalty and commitment have to become established.

Another aspect of the societal context of economic organizations which has been emphasized by Hamilton and Biggart (1988) is the role of the state in developing industrialization and the part played by different elite groups in that process. The lack of strong state involvement in the British industrial revolution has clearly affected the development of British enterprises and their relation to the financial system (Ingham, 1984) just as the role of the Japanese and South Korean states has strongly affected the emergence of zaibatsu and chaebol and their subsequent development. In addition to the extent of state involvement in developing industrialization and the willingness of dominant groups to accept, for instance, land reform and the legitimacy of state direction and coordination, the ability of state agencies to mobilize commitments and organize economic activities throughout a society is clearly a crucial factor in determining the dominant pattern of economic organization and indeed, a "hard" state in this sense has been seen as a critical ingredient in the successful industrialization of developing countries (Jones and Sakong, 1980).

Allied to the critical role of the state is the general pattern of elite group formation in a society and its commitment to productive resource coordination and control as the prime means of acquiring and maintaining power and privilege. Where dominant groups prefer and/or are encouraged to prefer state employment, rentier roles or commercial activities to developing and controlling large export market oriented economic enterprises, it is unlikely that integrated industrial groups will become established or industrialists acquire high social prestige. Equally, they are unlikely to develop a high degree of cultural self-confidence and willingness to invest large resources for long term growth strategies.

These aspects of the societal contexts of economic actors can be listed as follows:

1. fundamental pattern of value orientation;
2. basis of authority and solidaristic groupings;
3. institutional pluralism and differentiation;
4. the extent of state direction of economic activity and its organization;
5. patterns of elite group formations and activities.

The second major set of characteristics of forms of economic resource coordination and control to be considered here is their organization of inter-enterprise linkages. Two broad continua can be distinguished: the degree of industrial specialization and the degree of formal coordination of enterprise policies and development by the state or other agencies. Each can be further subdivided, for instance in horizontal and vertical specialization. As part of the first continuum, it is necessary to take account of the typical scope of economic activities within which "firms" restrict themselves. Examples here might be the Chinese family business which is normally highly specialized in one product-market, compared to a typically diversified Western corporation. A further aspect is the degree to which administrative coordination systems overlap with and/or are connected in different ways to resource allocation and direction systems. Are "firms" at the same time genuinely cohesive and bounded financial and legal units as well as management units?

The second continuum reflects the nature of the collaboration and cooperation within an array of economic actors. One might for instance cite the fairly high degree of hierarchical and formal coordination processes orchestrated by the Korean government between the chaebol and their constituent parts. This contrasts with post-war Japan where the work of MITI is equally hierarchical but much less formal, and with Hong Kong where no coordination is designed hierarchically or formally in the society and any inter-enterprise collaboration is left to informal processes among the actors at the base. This continuum also reflect horizontal linkages such as cartels and cross-shareholdings leading to coordinated strategies and decisions as in bank coordination, industrial groups etc..

When looking inside the economic unit, it becomes difficult to reduce the categories to less than three continua and thus a three-dimensional space. Bearing in mind that the legally defined firm is not necessarily the unit of analysis, and that these terms should not be interpreted via the language of traditional organization theory, three major continua are (i) the formalization of control, (ii) the degree and methods of subunit integration, (iii) the centralization of authority.

The formalization of control is a complex dimension consisting of more than formalization itself. It is a vector containing:

1. the nature of authority and mode of commitment;
2. the degree of formalization of procedures and relationships;
3. role specificity and differentiation of sub-units;
4. the reproductivity and stability of an impersonal social structure independent of individuals; and
5. reliance on specialized managerial competence for recruitment to top managerial posts.

The degree of sub-unit integration assumes a continuum of coordination methods which are cumulative, beginning with sub-contracting, then adding personal (kin) relations, then hierarchy, then a strong emphasis on the corporate culture. Analysis of this continuum incorporates information about the nature of the dominant organizational units used for the carrying out of tasks. This means taking into account their size, the nature of their boundaries, types of tasks subsumed, and the fundamental basis of differentiation (e.g., phase of material transformation, system functions, output).

Centralization of authority reflects the dominant authority principles of the society, and incorporates information about the distinguishing characteristics of top management, its modus operandi, and the methods whereby such power comes to be allocated.

A summary of the constraints of the various continua is provided in Table 7.1. This makes a separation between the broad continua, their main constituents, and the empirical referents whereby their workings may come to be understood.

Table 7.1 *Continua for Characterizing Economic Actors*

Continua	Constituents	Empirical referents
Intra-Enterprise		
1. Formaliza-tion of Control	Impersonality of relationships	Nature of authority and mode of commitment. Neutrality, objectivity of procedures. Nepotism
	Formalization of procedures	Degree of bureaucratization
	Differentiation	Role specificity, specialization and differentiation. Specialized managerial competence
2. Sub-unit integration	Coordination of sub-units	Extent to which sub-units are systema-tically integrated
		Methods of integration e.g., contractual, personal (kin), hierarchy, corporate culture
	Unit formation	Size, boundaries, types of tasks subsumed
		Fundamental basis of differentation (material transformation, systems function, output)
3. Centraliza-tion	Dominant coalition	Characteristics of top management
		Operating methods
		Way power is allocated
	Authority principle	Dominant form of social cohesion
		Organizational units of identity

Table 7.1 *Continua for Characterizing Economic Actors (cont'd)*

Continua	Constituents	Empirical referents
Inter-Enterprise		
1. Industrial specialization	Organizational scope	Organizational concentration on one product/market
	Linkages across sectors	Nature of links with other companies
	Boundary concordance	Overlap with resource allocation and directing systems
2. Coordination across actors	Hierarchical coordination	Strength of gov't guidance. Strength of conglomerate guidance e.g., Keiretsu, Bank control.
	Horizontal coordination	Cartelization
		Cross-shareholdings
		Interlocking directorates, Means of coordinating input-output markets

7.3.1 The Emergence of Stable Patterns

In order to illustrate the working of this analysis we propose to take the recipes which appear stable and decipher their constituent parts. This will then allow for some arguments to be presented about linkages to contextual factors.

As a five-dimensional space is not feasible for normal discourse, we propose to consider the economic actors in terms of the two dimensions of inter-enterprise analysis and the three dimensions in intra-enterprise analysis. This provides the conceptual framework given in Figure 7.1, and in this we have hypothesized the positions taken by the Chinese family business network, the chaebol and the zaibatsu .

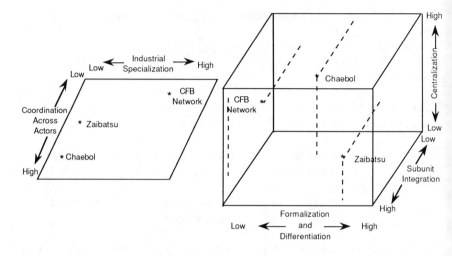

Figure 7.1 *Elements of a typology of economic coordination and control*

7.3.2 The Example of the Chinese Family Business

The Chinese family business is a dominant economic form in the Overseas Chinese diaspora of East and Southeast Asia. It accounts for much of the competitiveness of the region and is found with a remarkably consistent pattern of behaviour in Taiwan, Hong Kong, Singapore, Philippines, Indonesia, Malaysia and Thailand.

Its characteristics normally follow a pattern which can be described thus:

1. small scale, and relatively simple organizational structuring;
2. normally focussed on one product or market;
3. centralized decision making with heavy reliance on one dominant executive;
4. a close overlap of ownership, control, and family;
5. a paternalistic organizational climate;
6. linked to the environment through personalistic networks;
7. normally very sensitive to matters of cost and financial efficiency;

8. commonly linked strongly but informally with related but legally independent organizations handling key functions such as parts supply or marketing;
9. relatively weak in terms of creating large-scale market recognition for brands;
10. a high degree of strategic adaptability.

Considering now the intra-organizational features of this type and how they may be related back to the societal context, centralization is typically high. This reflects two main features of that context, (a) the dominant authority principle and (b) the degree of trust. In the case of Chinese culture (traditional Chinese culture being preserved among the Overseas Chinese), the hierarchical principles of the Confucian social order provide a strong tendency for benevolent autocracy to be a widely accepted organizing principle. That this functions relatively smoothly is an indication of the extent of socialization and also the extent to which leaders, by accepting the obligations of paternalism as well as its rights, succeed in establishing widely accepted formulae for compliance.

The element of trust in Chinese society is perhaps better understood as a problem of mistrust. One of the legacies of Chinese history is the need for family units to rely on their own resources for supporting the survival and prosperity of members. This leads to an essentially competitive set of societal units, each responsible for its own economic well-being. In this atmosphere trust cannot be assumed, and instead operates on the basis of very specific bonds which are personalistic and cemented by mutual obligation. Societal norms support more widespread communal co-operativeness (Lau, 1982; Silin, 1976; Fei, 1948). The head of a family business, in his role as steward of family resources, and normally with dominant ownership of the organization, finds it difficult for reasons of mistrust to release information on a sufficient scale to foster delegated decision making, and this brake on decentralization also contributes to the maintenance of the pattern of small scale benevolent autocracies.

Formalization and differentiation in Chinese family businesses are normally low, partly reflecting organizational size limitations but also a more personalistic approach to the co-operative process. There is also a contribution to the diminution of formal control from the societal predisposition to accept authority and its consequence, that is, a lower need for institutionalized discipline processes.

Sub-unit integration is at the centre of the concerns in this paper, in that we are advocating a unit of analysis for understanding economic activity which in many cases extends beyond the boundaries of the firm as legal entity. In the Overseas Chinese case, products and services reach the market as a result of coalitions of separate family businesses acting together but casing that action not on legal contractual ties but on ties of informally coordinated mutual benefit. This is the means whereby the size limitations are surmounted. An owner dominated organization, unable to delegate power, will be unable to control many functions within itself if they become complex. It can, however, be part of a larger construct. A factory for instance can function like a production department. A shipping and forwarding agent can function like a transport department. A sourcing company can function like a buying department. The informal networking of a series of family businesses can function as the equivalent, to the large, integrated bureaucracy in terms of economic coordination and control.

The question thus arises: what is the unit and what is the subunit? If we apply the principle that the end-result of economic resource so-ordination and control is the creation of a product or service, then the unit of analysis for the Overseas Chinese case is a network of small organizations, something termed by Redding and Tam (1985) the molecular organization, in order to capture the idea of a set of connected principles.

Under this definition the integration of such units is at a low degree of formality. Firms move in and out of the arrangement according to market forces. At the same time, because of the high value attached to mutual obligation, the system has more inherent stability in this society than might be the case elsewhere. Integration is thus capable of working effectively without contractual ties or hierarchy.

The integration process, based as it is on personalistic bonding, reflects Chinese behavioural forms about specific friendship ties, in turn deriving from Confucian teaching. These act as the basis for the reduction of uncertainty in economic transactions and allow the general problem of mistrust to be handled adequately.

There are arguably connections between the three dimensions of this matrix. An organization which is low on formalization and differentiation, and thus tending to be high on more personalistic means of control, is likely at the same time to be highly centralized. Without the formalization of organizational processes it is difficult to maintain predictability of action if decentralization takes place. At the same time, if personalism is the principle means of achieving coordination between the subunits of the economic resource coordination system (i.e. separate family business closely focused on specific functions) then that system may be taken to have a medium-to-high score on coordination. The force of centralization will play a part here because of the power attached to the head of the organization. Coordination becomes a matter of connections between "all-powerful" individuals and as long as those connections are mutually beneficial, Chinese social norms will ensure their stability and reliability.

At the inter-organizational level of analysis, two principle dimensions interact, namely (a) industrial specialization, and (b) coordination between units of economic action. In an economy dominated by Chinese family business a high level of specialization occurs. This is largely due to the limitations on the variety which can be handled by groups of centralized, small-scale organizations, and a link thus exists with the intra-organizational features. This tendency to specialize is also strongly influenced by the societal problem of trust. The relative inability to trust others is partly counteracted by specific bonds of personalistic trust, but these are limited in their range simply by the amount of interpersonal bridging work required to maintain them. The erection of alternative coordination systems of a more classically bureaucratic nature, involving neutral, objective, contractual relations appears to be resisted in this culture. These limitations have to be lived with, and the principle response in doing so is the restriction of complexity, and thus the holding on to specialized concentration.

Coordination between organizations in most of the economies in which the Overseas Chinese flourish is at a low level. Such coordination as is sponsored by government bodies, or trade associations in other cultures such as Japan or Korea, is normally absent in the laissez-faire atmospheres of Taiwan and Hong Kong. In the Philippines, Thailand and Malaysia, the Overseas Chinese are normally working at some distance from government control, and so are the majority of Chinese companies in Indonesia. Singapore displays somewhat more government influence than the average, but there are still not high levels of inter-organizational coordination achieved there, at least in the Chinese-owned sector.

It could be argued that this reflects both the dominant authority principle of the society and the normal basis of loyalty. In the Chinese case, government control over business was always to be escaped if possible, as the attitude of traditional Chinese governments was to extort from the business sector and to treat its members as being of low status. Almost nothing was done actively to promote business, and organizations traditionally looked defensively to their own interests. This had an incidental side effect in that large scale implied visibility and thus vulnerability.

The basis of loyalty in these circumstances was the family firm, or for the non-family member the paternalistic, familistic atmosphere of a firm. In matters economic, the state has never in the Chinese case been seen as a legitimate coordinator. The contrasting cases of Japan and Korea are dramatic.

The end result is that the sponsoring of coordination in the Overseas Chinese case is very difficult and rarely attempted. An illustrative case is the Taiwanese government's attempt to sponsor a sophisticated plastics industry with large firms. The end result was one very large firm and 3,500 very small ones (Hamilton and Biggart, 1988).

It is clear that this low degree of coordination is in part a function of the huge number of small units which would need to be coordinated to produce, say, the Chinese equivalent of a *zaibatsu,* a *chaebol,* or a Western conglomerate. The practical difficulties of negotiating with so many decision-makers are clearly immense. In a broader sense, intense specialization by its nature negates high levels of inter-organizational coordination.

7.3.3 The Role of the Pattern-variables

So far, in analyzing the societal factors which appear to relate to the form of organization used by the overseas Chinese to coordinate and control economic behaviour, we have reached back only to the manifestation of deeper cultural traits, rather than the cultural traits themselves. In discussing authority principles, bases of identity, principles of cooperation, we have left unsaid what, in turn lies underneath them. Hence there is a need to go deeper, at least briefly and speculatively into the pattern variables which determine the values manifest in action.

Affectivity is more normal in Chinese culture than affective neutrality and it supports the obligation exchange implicit in the dominant authority principles of paternalism. It also acts to consolidate the networks of personalism, and in doing so, acts as a barrier to the more affectively neutral bureaucratic type of relations.

A collectivity orientation is more normal than self-orientation for the Chinese (Hofstede, 1980; Redding and Richardson, 1986), and in particular the collectivity of family. The salience of the collectivity is also visible in the tendency to affiliate with proto-family groups such as paternalistically managed institutions, and also the rules for maintaining collectivities inspire the stability of relationship networks beyond the work or family group.

Particularism as opposed to universalism is visible in the non-development of bureaucracy and also the somewhat unpredictable processes of indigenous Chinese law (although it must be acknowledged that colonial influences have meant that purely indigenous Chinese law is rarely visible in the Overseas Chinese area). Abstract notions of organizational rationality are, however, also less developed than in Western or Japanese cases and may reflect the dominance of particularistic mental frameworks, which prefer ad hoc decision processes and personalistic assessments.

Ascription is one of the determinants of the personalism already noted, and by the same token, the lack of access to more objective achievement based judgements of people is one of the barriers which inhabit the emergence of bureaucracies.

The question of specificity-diffuseness yields very subtle subsidiary questions about mental processes, but descriptions of Chinese cognition (Nakamura, 1964; Needham, 1956; Northrop, 1960) suggest that diffuseness is more typical than specificity. In this case, there are arguably connections with the somewhat more nebulous systems of building organizations and their more fluid internal and external relationships and structures.

It is not proposed to explore in detail the workings of the *zaibatsu* or *chaebol,* but a number of fairly obvious distinguishing features may be outlined in order to illustrate the main variances which the model would be expected to illuminate. One of the clearest distinctions is that drawn by Hamilton and Biggart (1988) in describing the locus of strategic decision-making, and thus the key point at which coordination is instigated to create economic action. In Korea they see this as resting mainly at the apex of society, and largely in the hands of government whose coalition with the heads of the *chaebols* is very close. In the case of Japan, it is seen as lying further down in the societal hierarchy, with a less clear state of collaboration between government and the heads of business. In the Overseas Chinese case, using Taiwan as an example, they argue it lies at the base of the economy, in the hands of the executives running the large number of small business. These three quite different societal formulae must inevitably play a part in the creation of the different forms of economic actor dominating in each society.

The *Zaibatsu,* re-formed after World War II in a manner which deliberately prevented the re-emergence of their pre-war family influenced predecessors, have acted as loosely coordinated coalitions. Trading among their members, borrowing and lending among themselves and their members, borrowing and lending among themselves and their hub banks, co-ordinated by a plethora of cross-directorships, they have sponsored beneficial cooperation while at the same time not preventing the exploration of innovative external linkages. Acting like a mutual benefit club, membership has not implied a great loss of autonomy since its central strategic role is visible (Clark, 1979). The entire body is built up of subtle connections, and yet, in the context of Japan can operate with a *de facto* cohesion which would not be possible in many other cultures given the apparent tenuousness of the connective tissue.

By contrast, the Korean *chaebol* is an instrument of the "hard state". The intentions of government, the implementing of the national plans, are conducted through these now immense structures, each working at the top very closely with a very business-oriented political power. At the same time, entrepreneurship and innovation is not stifled, and in fact this unique formulae is a means of maximizing the use of entrepreneurship talent which, at a crucial stage of fast development, was in relatively short supply. It would appear that the *chaebol* is a more obviously integrated and coordinated structure than the *zaibatsu,* and also that it has a clearer hierarchy within it. Their superficial similarities are thus deceptive (Jones and Sakong, 1980).

Within the "post-Confucian" area generally, therefore, three radically different forms of dominant economic actor exists. Although they all contain patterns of relationships and behaviour which can be traced back to largely Confucian societal values, the variation in the way such values become manifest is great. More significantly perhaps, the contrast of any of the three with the Western bureaucracy is very clear, no more so than in the definition of the boundaries within which economic action is coordinated and controlled.

7.4 Implications

The approach proposed here is inevitable tentative, given the paucity of empirical studies addressing the issue. It is also inevitably contentious as it crosses the boundaries of a number of normally discrete intellectual fields, the main ones being organization theory, economics, sociology, political science, and social psychology. The dangers of both of these weaknesses are readily acknowledged. However, the need for a multi-disciplinary approach in matters of high complexity, the ethnocentrism of much of the core theory in economics and organization studies, and the critical need for more theoretically coherent and comprehensive taxonomies, imply some such comparative framework.

The value of taxonomies which can foster comparison hardly need justification as a mean of advancing understanding. The need for research to be guided by more focused questions is apparent as so many cross-cultural studies replicated each other and appear to take the discipline round in hermeneutic circles (Adler, 1983). To break out of such circles requires occasional thinking at a tangent to what is normal. This attempt to question the notion of the key unit of analysis for studying economic action is just such a tangential approach. It breaks from an important norm and is done in the interests of a more constructive shift of the paradigm for comparative management and related studies.

In this paper, we have illustrated the approach with an Asian example to illuminate the core point. This is that the emergence of such different recipes, each in its particular and temporal set of surrounding conditions, produces economic institutions of comparable effectiveness when it comes to performance in world markets. The understanding of that effectiveness, and all the questions of replicability which are allied to it, is contingent on some understanding of those surrounding conditions. In this process of understanding there is no more crucial point to deal with than the definition of the basic unit of analysis for the study of economic action.

7.5 References

Abegglen, J. and G. Stalk, (1987). *Kaisha.* New York: Basic Books.

Adler, N.J. (1983). Cross-cultural Management Research: The Ostrich and the Trend. *Academy of Management Review,* 8, 2, 226–232

Bauer, M. and E. Cohen (1981). *Qui Gouverne les Groupes Industriels?.* Paris: Seuil.

Callon, M. and J.-P. Vignolle (1977). Breaking Down the Organization. *Social Science Information,* 16, 2, 147–167.

Chandler, A.D. (1981). Historical Determinants of Managerial Hierarchies. In A. van den Ven and W.F. Joyce (eds.), *Perspectives on Organization Design and Behavior,* New York: Wiley, 291–402.

Clark, R. (1979). *The Japanese Company.* New Haven: Yale University Press.

Daems, H. (1983). The Determinants of the Hierarchical Organization of Industry, in A. Francis, J. Turk and P. Williams (eds.), *Power Efficiency and Institutions.* London: Heinemann, 35–53.

Fei, X. T. (1948). *Rural China.* Shanghai: Guancha She.

Hamilton, G. and N.W. Biggart (1988). Market, Culture and Authority: A Comparative Analysis of Management and Organization in the Far East. *American Journal of Sociology, Special Supplement on the Sociology of the Economy,* 33–51.

Hofheinz, R. and K.E. Calder (1982) *The East Asia Edge.* New York: Basic Books.

Hofstede, G. (1980). *Cultures consequences.* London: Sage Publications.

Ingham, G.(1984). *Capitalism Divided.* London: Macmillan.

Jones, L.P. and I. Sakong (1980). *Government, Business and Entrepreneurship in Economic Development: the Korean case.* Cambridge, MA: Harvard University Press.

Kahn, H. (1979). *World Economic Development: 1979 and Beyond.* London: Croon Helm.

Lau, S.K. (1982). *Society and Politics in Hong Kong.* Hong Kong: Chinese University Press.

Locke, R. (1984). *The End of the Practical Man.* Greenwich, CT: JAI Press.

Nakamura, H. (1964). *Ways of Thinking of Eastern peoples.* Honolulu: University of Hawaii Press.

Needham, J. (1956). *Science and Civilization in China, Vol. 2.* Cambridge, England: Cambridge University Press.

Northrop, F.S.C. (1960). *The Meeting of East and West.* New York: Macmillan.

Parsons, T. (1951). *The Social System.* New York: The Free Press.

Penrose, E.T. (1959). *The Theory of the Growth of the Firm.* Oxford: Blackwell.

Redding, S.G. and S. Richardson (1986). Participative Management and Its Varying Relevance in Hong Kong and Singapore, *Asia Pacific Journal of Management,* 3(2), 76–98.

Redding, S.G. and S.K.W. Tam (1985). Networks and Molecular Organizations: An Exploratory View of Chinese Firms in Hong Kong, in K.C. Mun and T.S. Chan (eds.) *Perspsectives in International Business.* Hong Kong: Chinese University Press, 129–142.

Silin, R. (1976). *Leadership and Values.* Cambridge, MA: Harvard University Press.

Williamson, O. (1975). *Markets and Hierarchies.* New York: Free Press.

8 Globalization: Separating the Fad from the Fact – Comments on the International Management Research Conference[1]

Henry Mintzberg
McGill University

An expert has been defined as a guy from out of town. Well, in this conference of international business people, I am not from out of the country but I am from out of the field.

An expert has also been defined as someone with no elementary knowledge. On this I qualify too. I travel a good deal but I know almost nothing about international business. I am interested in organizations, wherever they happen to function.

And then an expert has been defined as someone who avoids all the many pitfalls on his or her way to the grand fallacy. I don't know about the pitfalls but I'll let you worry about the fallacy.

I shall address three issues: why global? what's global? what consequence global?

8.1 Why Global?

As international business people, you seem to wear your biases rather openly. You are unabashed lobbyists, champions for the types of organizations you study. Almost everything I heard here portrayed international business in a positive light and the internationalization of business as a wonderful thing. Yves Doz made a comment about "for better or worse", adding "My own view is better". And I heard Steve Kobrin's presentation

---

[1] This chapter is a text rendition of notes I put together quickly during the conference, in response to what I heard, to be presented as a commentary. The ideas are not well developed – I present them at the editors' request, more for stimulation than for conclusion.

as testament to the glories of internationalization (ironic, perhaps, given what I found out about Steve's background later, but as one prominent member of the audience quipped, maybe I really did hear correctly).

In any event, this worries me, for obvious reasons. I shall consider some problems of internationalization, social and political as well as economic, later. Let me just note here that I listen to all of this as a citizen of Canada, where the glories of the great multinational world of business have often amounted to a euphemism for economic colonialism. You don't have to spend your time putting down internationalization, that would undermine your efforts, but please, a little more balance.

That's the bad news. The good news is that I think your focus on international business benefits you greatly, in a particular respect that is otherwise killing business schools today. What struck me at this conference, especially in contrast to most other academic ones I attend, is how pragmatic has been the discussion. Part of this must be attributed to Fritz and Durhane, who I think have organized it wonderfully. But I sense that this is also intrinsic to the field, and it occurred to me while listening that this may be as for a very special reason.

What I think is killing the business schools today is that most of their thinking and research is *driven by concepts,* at worst concepts rooted in the base disciplines of mathematics, economics, and psychology, rather than in something about organizations themselves. In other words, it is abstractions that drive the work rather than something in the real experiences of organizations. What we have is the "rule of the tool" with a vengeance: People are running around half cocked looking for places to impose the latest "in" in the theoretical world, whether it be agency theory or game theory or expert systems rooted in some half-baked ideas about the programming of human cognition. (Funny how a machine that does nothing more than move electrical impulses around rather quickly has so enraptured us.) This, I believe, is fundamentally corrupting for any applied field but especially ours, one of Simon's "artificial" sciences,which should be pulled by problems instead of pushed by concepts.

Perhaps God created Americans to test theories. Is so, she never dreamed that there would be so many Americans and so few theories worth testing. I believe research in management should be driven far more than it is now by questions to be answered, not by hypotheses to be tested.

It occurred to me listening to the discussion here that what keeps you pragmatic is that you have a particular constituency in mind. Championing the needs of international business may bias you, but it also focuses your attention on a client, someone who consumes you products (namely the insights of your research) for productive ends. And that's a very healthy mind set to have, especially when many of your colleagues in finance (read economics or mathematics) and organizational behavior (read psychology), etc. (not strategy, not yet!) have been flying in ever diminishing circles and are in the process of disappearing up their own rear ends. So ignore all those phoney calls for "rigor", you have better things to do than impress some snot-nosed professor in the faculty club, and get on with answering interesting questions for your clients.

8.2   What's Global?

A lot less than you believe, I believe. The label is too "in", the concept too woolly. Someone I know once said that "everyone has two cars", everyone she knew anyway. Well, sometimes I think your idea of the globe is a swath that cuts across the middle of the northern hemisphere, starting, say in Seattle and continuing around to about Vienna, then skipping across to about Hong Kong and ending up in Tokyo. Everyone *you* know seems to be found there. There is huge world out there beyond Schiphol Airport and the Tokyo Hilton, even in Japan let alone Sri Lanka or the Ozarks. Culture has been stressed by Nancy Adler at this conference. Well, the yuppiedom of international academia (and business) forms its own isolated culture too – "global ethnocentricity" we might call it.

In fact, it would be helpful to differentiate different types of "global" producers, as Gordon Redding called for here (and helped by describing the particular brand of family organization to the overseas Chinese). There are, of course, those firms that do market virtually globally, the Coca Cola's of this world. But they are a special type, dispensing their marketing and sometime manufacturing functions but hardly letting go of product development and design, for example. But I don't think this is what international business people have in mind today when they use the term global. This type might still be the most significant but it is no longer the most enticing. The type of organization that I suspect sits in those minds is what I prefer to call the "international rationalizer". IBM has long been an example of this (in production; its marketing is more global), but I prefer to use IKEA, which designs its furniture in Scandinavia, sources much of it in Eastern Europe, and sells it in Western Europe and America. Hardly the globe, but interestingly international. Unlike the rest of this field of management, in scholarship no less than in practice, you would do well to question excessively popular concepts that are themselves too global.

8.3 What Consequence Global?

Let me come to that bias, because Yves, I think it's for worse as well as far better. I heard comments here about the benefits of public states responding to private enterprises, but hardly the opposite, also implications about local control as an impediment to efficient production. All this worries me. The latter may be true in the narrowest sense of efficiency, but who wants that kind of efficiency? And what about social factors, problems of Schumacher's one dimensional man, the need to stimulate local culture, the advantages of differentiation. (Imagine being able to get off an aeroplane in Tokyo and having a sense that you are somewhere different!) When national boundaries give way, will we all have to reduce America's health-care system, to Japan's watchman's, to Italy's styles, to England's punk musicians? Tailoring Campbell Soup to local tastes is hardly my idea of the wonders of the global village. If that's what you mean by global, I'll take a little more domestic, eh.

I remember years ago, the surprising finding in a study by Simmonds, again during a time when we were being inundated with stories of the wonders of "geocentricity" as they called it in those days, that only 13 of the 3,847 top managers of the 150 largest U.S. corporations were foreign nationals transferred from foreign operations to their positions at headquarters. All the rest were American nationals, save a handful of foreigners who came to America at young ages and worked their way up. In other words, M. Maisonrouge, the French national in the executive suite of IBM then, the very archetype of the very modern geocentric manager, turned out to be an oddity, the exception that falsified the rule. Is Mr. O'Reilly, the Irish national who now runs Heinz, still that sort of oddity? Whose global village is it going to be anyway?

How multilingual, for example, are those American business people and academics who circle their "globe" calling for internationalism? Maybe we should listen more carefully when the international business professors can themselves achieve a truly international society for international business, balanced between the Europeans and the Americans. (The Academy of Management, making lots of noises about internationalization of late, cannot even bring itself to hold its annual conference abroad. Apparently so foreign a place as Montreal, was rejected on the grounds that there would not be enough airline access. Come up by dogsled and have a look, guys!)

Why is no-one discussing the obvious dangers of joint ventures? When all those big dinosaurs, the "global" business together with their partner local governments, merge into one big cozy network, who will look after competition? And eclecticism? And the realities of entrepreneurship, as opposed to the promises of intrapreneurship? If we really do achieve the global integration that now seems so popular, who will be left to control things? The outlook for international government is hardly bright, yet will that not have to rise up as a countervailing power? Then we shall have a true bureaucracy, supporting truly global totalitarianism on the outside, true politicization on the inside.

Well, enough of my half-baked ideas. In making my case for parochialism, I turn out not to be a guy from out of town. And I have certainly revealed my lack of elementary knowledge. I don't even know enough to separate my pitfalls from my fallacy. But I do hope I have been able to put a pin into your global balloon so that you can see it for what it really might be, for better and for worse.

9 Research in International Business: A Canadian Perspective

Alan M. Rugman
University of Toronto

9.1 Introduction

Canadian researchers of international business live in one of the world's most exciting laboratories. With about 30 percent of Canada's output being exported and a high degree of economic and financial integration with the United States, Canada has one of the most open systems in the global economy. Virtually every manager in Canada is influenced by international events in business and finance. This means that the study of business in Canada is really the study of international business.

Yet in business schools across Canada, and in the related fields of law economics, political science and other social sciences, much of Canadian thinking and research is still dominated by models of large, closed and self-sufficient systems rather than the small, open economy relevant for Canadian business. Even in the relatively new field of international business, much of the research has been adapted from U.S. thinking, leading to a neglect of important issues relevant for Canadian managers.

Canadian based researchers need to develop new theory and analysis which will be relevant in the training of a new generation of Canadian managers. For example, a key field of research, of great relevance for Canadian managers, is global strategic management. In Canada, a strategic approach to the problems of international business cannot be copied from the Harvard Business School. The Canadian manager must be well informed about the nature of the economic and policy environment affecting his or her business in Canada, not the United States. The Canadian manager must wrestle with both conceptual issues and practical problems in designing suitable strategic responses to changes in environmental parameters. The solutions will not necessarily be the same as those adopted by a U.S. manager.

For example, the Canadian manager must be keenly aware of aspects of recent Canadian trade and investment policy. When major changes in policy come about, for example, the negotiation and signing of the Canada-U.S. free trade agreement in the 1986–1988 period, then managers must react quickly. The art of management demands successful strategic thinking, coupled with structural methods to implement new corporate strategies. In the changing world environment facing Canadian managers the need for a relevant approach to business becomes more apparent every day.

9.2 The Policy Relevance of International Business

The debate on free trade in the Canadian federal election of 1988 was an example of the relevance of international business as a key field of study in Canada. For several weeks the Canadian electorate publicly debated the substance of issues such as global competition, strategies of multinational enterprises, foreign ownership, rules of origin and value added criteria, subsidies, trade law, harmonization and the alleged trade-off between political sovereignty and economic integration.

The meetings of the General Agreement on Tariffs and Trade (GATT) in Montreal, in December 1988, again illustrated the overwhelming and seminal influence of international business topics on the policy agenda of Canada and other nations. Dispute settlement, agricultural subsidies, trade in services and intellectual property, trade-related investment measures and related topics were debated by business groups, governments and think tanks. What was once the esoteric preserve of pasty-faced trade bureaucrats and bespectacled professors was now front page news in Canada and a topic for television and radio discussion.

The Corporate Higher Education Forum in Canada recently released a major study called Going Global: Meeting the Need for International Business Expertise in Canada. This identifies the need for much greater interaction and cooperation between the three key players in the development of international business knowledge: the universities, business and governments. The Forum concluded that without such cooperation Canada's future economic prosperity would be compromised.

Given this demonstrated public interest in international business in Canada we need to question the development of the scholarly literature in this field on purely academic terms; research must be relevant for managers. International business in Canada is an emerging field where good scholarly research has an immediate application in the formulation of business strategy and government policy. Much of the best academic thinking is already reflected, or is being incorporated into, business plans and government documents. In this survey, therefore, the major issues in the field of international business will be identified. The issues highlighted reflect the author's experience and judgement as a leader in the development of the field of international business in Canada and as a senior participant in the negotiations for the Canada-U.S. Free Trade Agreement as the only academic member of the International Trade Advisory Committee for 1986–1988.

Examples of research output and notable authors in this field can be found in the annual proceedings of the International Business Division of the Administrative Science Association of Canada (ASAC). In addition, a number of Canadian-based scholars publish in the leading field publication, the Journal of International Business Studies, and several Canadians are members of its Editorial Board, or of the Executive of the sponsoring Academy of International Business. Canadian scholars also publish in a variety of related academic and professional outlets and contribute to research paper series organized by the six publicly funded international business centers and other international policy research groups across Canada.

9.3 Research Themes in International Business in Canada

Research in international business today and in the future involves the analysis of the trade and investment aspects of international exchange. The focus of much research work and specialist training in this field is the multinational enterprise and its functional areas – research and development, production, marketing, human resource management, and finance. This includes the analysis of the international environment and corporate strategic planning. The special problems of small and medium-sized business also need to be addressed, with particular attention to entrepreneurship and export marketing opportunities.

As the multinational enterprise operates in a system of regulation it is necessary to understand the interaction between the legal environment and corporate strategies; such an interaction is of interest to private sector managers, corporate lawyers, public policy analysts, trade unionists, consumers and the community at large.

Research needs to address both international trade and direct invest-ment and the important interaction of the two. For example, in today's complex economy, more than 70% of all Canadian trade with the United States is intra-firm trade within multinational enterprises. It is also notable that current issues in Canada-U.S. relations are as much concerned with foreign investment as with trade.

Due to the controversial nature of multinational enterprises, and the power that they wield, it is also necessary to examine the nature of cor-porate social responsibility and the manner in which multinational enter-prises interact with governments, regulatory agencies, and international organizations.

Researchers today need to interact with, and have access to, the leading business and financial institution, trade councils and consulates of Euro-pean and Asian nations. It is necessary for business faculty to work along with the private sector in developing major new research projects to an-alyze the nature of multinational enterprises and their relationship to fe-deral and provincial government policies.

It is well known that the problem of U.S. protectionism and the decen-tralized nature of the U.S. system of government constitute challenges for companies doing business there. With the Canada-U.S. free trade agree-ment in place, the substantive nature of business strategies and their re-lationship with government and investment policy need to be researched. Related topics in the areas of international competitiveness, foreign ownership, world product mandating, technology transfer, and financial management in a a world of exchange risk also need to be examined from a distinctly Canadian perspective.

Both in the bilateral trade agreement and in the present multilateral "Uruguay round" of the GATT the issues of trade in services are impor-tant. Services raise complicated and politically sensitive questions of fo-reign investment, transfer of technology, and mobility of persons associa-ted with the installation and development of such services. Canadians are particularly well placed to study these phenomena as they are both im-porters and exporters of technology and capital. Considerably more work needs to be done to make the Canadian business and academic commun-ities aware of the competitive advantages which we may have in many of these fields and provide them with the necessary expertise to exploit that advantage in the export market.

Research in international business needs to involve both people who have previously done research in these areas and those whose research, while initially in other areas or disciplines, is applicable to new challenges and opportunities posed to Canada by a changing trade environment. While faculty members teaching international business in Canadian business schools can provide a nucleus for such research, faculty from other disciplines, both in Canada and abroad, business and labor leaders, and public sector personnel must be encouraged and invited to participate in such research.

It is necessary to identify projects which address the weaknesses in Canada's international competitive position identified by the International Management forum and others. For example a project on accelerating the diffusion of new technology in Canadian business could address Canada's weaknesses in updating product and production techniques.

9.4   Future Research Topics: A Canadian Perspective

In an integrated global economic and business system it is necessary for scholars from smaller nations such as Canada to develop their own theories about international business. A major intellectual effort is required over the next ten years to build a distinctive field of study in Canada which is relevant for Canadian managers.

This fundamental thinking will require an understanding of the limitations of theories developed by academic colleagues for economic superpowers such as Japan and the United States. Many of these theories do not apply to smaller countries like Canada, the Newly Industrialized Countries (NIC's mostly smaller European nations and third world countries. Example of current mistaken applications include:

1. strategic trade policy, since small, open economies cannot afford protectionism;
2. administration of trade remedy laws, since the definition of subsidy is biased toward larger economies;
3. poor strategic management, since the impact of triad power requires access by a small nation of the markets of a member of the triad.
4. parent-subsidiary relationships, since the two way flows of direct investment now make smaller nations like Canada the home of large multinationals;
5. ethnocentric management attitudes towards host nations, since the United States, like most European nations, is now a leading host nation for direct investment;

6. blinkered human resource management practices, since the increasing autonomy of subsidiaries requires greater cultural awareness.

In these, and related, areas it is clearly insufficient to understand and adapt "mainstream" thinking in international business. Instead, it is necessary to do some new thinking. This research will result in modifications and testing of internalization theory, since the use of intermediate forms of activity like networks and cooperative ventures is increasing, yet some of these may be culture-specific and not generalize to other systems. It will be aided by process research, analyzing the 200 largest multinationals in the triad which account for 80% of international business. It will be based upon topics debated in the Canada-U.S. Free trade Agreement, and in the GATT, where Canadian concerns about subsidies, dispute settlement, investment policies and related issues become the focus of public attention.

Canadians have made a start. The following section summarizes a survey of Canadian academic research on International Business made by Stephen Luxmore. The bibliography on which it is based is available from the editors. Of the seventeen journals researched for contributions relevant to the international business topics discussed above, well over 200 articles were identified. Much work remains to be done in transforming many of these ideas from the academic to the practical realm. Indeed, it would appear that Canadian researchers are not as much lacking in their academic research ability as in their willingness to be practical and disseminate new information to professional groups. This is a structural and organizational problem which is clearly capable of solution.

9.5 Survey of Canadian Research Articles[1]

A survey of recent articles appearing in Canadian, American and International journals indicates the direction of current research in international business in Canada or concerning Canadian business issues. The criteria for inclusion were as follows: 1) the author is Canadian based/funded; or 2) the research is published in a Canadian journal; or 3) the article's focus is on a Canadian issue, whether it be business, government or trade.

---

[1] This section of the chapter was prepared by Stephen Luxmore.

As with most academic research the majority of the literature search was confined to journals and scholarly books. Comments and notes in journals were not included. Further, several important sources were missed, such as publications of the C.D. Howe Institute and other Canadian research organizations. Table 9.1 identifies the journals by major and minor focus. Major focus journals are those which were searched directly; minor focus journals were those in which an author or subject was searched.

Table 9.1 *Journals Included in Survey of Canadian International Business Research*

Major Focus	Minor Focus
Business Quarterly (1984)	American Economic Review
Canadian Journal of Economics (1984)	American Review of Canadian Studies
Canadian Public Policy (1984)	Canadian Journal of Administrative Studies
Journal of International Business Studies (1978)	Columbia Journal of World Business
Management International Review (1984)	Economic Letters
	European Economic Review
	International Journal of Industrial Organization
	Journal of Economic Behavior and Organization
	Journal of International Money and Finance
	Journal of Political Economy
	Journal of World Trade Law
	Managerial and Decision Economics

The literature was placed within one of the categories listed in table 9.2, with the recognition that many articles could be classified in more than one category.

Table 9.2 *Classification of Canadian Research Articles According to Research Topics*

Category	Number of Entries
Business/Government Relations and Free Trade	22
International Economics	28
International Finance	7
Multinational Enterprises and the Theory of the MNE	26
Organizational Behavior	3
Strategy	30

Under the Business/Government Relations and Free Trade classification we observed that the majority of articles concern the Canadian-American Free Trade Agreement and its impact upon the Canadian economy. In this survey, few authors have addressed business/government interaction, such as export support or specifics like administration of trade remedy laws or GATT trade issues.

The articles classified as belonging to International Economics also had free trade as a major emphasis, but these papers were economic, rather than business or Canada-U.S. Free Trade Agreement focused. Many economists recognized the difficulties facing business restricted to a small market for they address international competitiveness as measured by productivity/capacity and scale economies, etc.. The relevance to International Business researchers is immediate – the significance of strategic trade policy in a small open economy and the requirement of access to a triad power economy.

The International Finance papers have a macro-economic approach to exchange rates and capital mobility. There remains room for specific analysis regarding the effects of exchange rate differentials upon international competitiveness and policy recommendations for interest rate and exchange rate targets.

The number of articles listed under Multinational Enterprises and the Theory of the MNE demonstrates the importance of the area to International Business researchers and the business community. There are several Canadian texts addressing International Business for use in the classroom. For the most part, the journal articles examine internationalization theory and expand its use from the previous applications to direct investment, to formally include joint ventures and licensing. There exists a requirement for more testing and application of the theory.

The low number of entries in the Organizational Behaviour category reflects the bias of the literature search towards economic oriented journals, rather than a lack of emphasis by Canadian scholars in this area. It does however illustrate the need for better integration of the two fields to facilitate the exchange of ideas and information.

The strategy category, which is best described as applied International Business, spans all the previously discussed classifications. International Business researchers have applied many of the economic based competitive studies to specific industries/firms with clear strategic implications for developing advantage. Business strategies and the Canada-U.S. Trade Agreement are examined in several articles and books. Cooperative ventures are addressed, as is export promotion. Further research is required in all areas, especially employing process methodologies.

10 International Management:
A Field in Transition –
What Will It Take To Reach Maturity

Edwin L. Miller
The University of Michigan

10.1 The Need for International Management Research

Business activity has become increasingly international and global, and firms are being challenged to develop a broader view of their mission. One consequence of the internationalization of business has been the emerging need for managers who have international expertise and an appreciation for the complexities of doing business in the global marketplace: managers who are mobile, adaptable, knowledgeable of different cultures, and capable of dealing effectively with people from these cultures (Kobrin, 1984). It follows that the international management field should have an important role to play in helping corporations and their managerial personnel compete in this highly competitive global marketplace. However, is the current body of knowledge and the research potential capable of providing scholars with theory, models and knowledge required for helping meet the problematic needs of corporations as well as advancing our understanding of the management process in different cultures and nations?

It is clear that we are now in the early stages of another "great leap forward" in the internationalization of the world's economic activity, and this has important implications for management worldwide. The world is rapidly moving toward blocs of nations in which the bloc becomes the focus rather than a particular country. New perspectives and models of analysis are beginning to emerge, and they pose unique challenges to corporate life and the management process. The strategy for penetrating the European Community, begun in 1992, is different from that for the penetration of a member nation. And the strategy for gaining access to members of the Asian bloc of nations or the North American bloc will be different still. Bloc and national protectionism, consumer demand, technological and managerial sophistication, and strategic alliances across borders are among some of the significant hurdles facing corporations as we move toward this new phase of the world's economic activity.

Are firms and their managements prepared to face this more competitive, more complex, and much harsher economic environment? According to Tung, many leading European and Japanese multinational firms place a very heavy emphasis on the company's international sales and operations, and they possess a global perspective toward their business (Tung, 1988). Although "international competitiveness" has become the shibboleth for U.S. business leadership as it copes with international competitors and global awareness, recent developments in the United States suggest that American business may be adopting policies and programs which are incompatible with the pursuit of global competitiveness. American corporations continue to lose market share to foreign competitors or are acquired by overseas firms.

There is a need to devise new strategies to compete successfully in this emerging, highly competitive bloc economy. Some global corporations have long prepared for this new world economy, but some have not. As business activity becomes increasingly global, firms and their managements, if they are to be successful, must come to understand that they will have to become global in their strategic perspective, their management decision making processes and their organization structures. Corporations will require managerial and technically-grounded staff who understand the complexities of managing and performing in a globally-oriented environment.

International management scholars and researchers have a responsibility for helping to prepare current and future members of management to lead today's organizations with tomorrow's knowledge. Are we as international management scholars and researchers prepared to meet these educational challenges? I believe that the answer is ambiguous, and that it will depend upon whom one is answering. It is not just a matter concerning the availability of international management courses or qualified faculty available to teach such courses. The heart of the issue is threefold: (1) it centers on the substance of the course content; (2) it must address the quality and rigor of international management research that adds to the development of international management theory and assists MNC's in the management process of their businesses; and (3) it requires knowledgeable faculty members capable of integrating research findings into management curriculum and management education programs.

Entrepreneurs, managers and technicians must develop a global view of the world in which they live and compete, and they must build confidence in their ability to compete successfully in the global marketplace. Business leaders will need to know more about other cultures: their value systems, their political and legal frameworks, and their economic systems. Language skills are acquiring a new urgency because the language acquisition becomes an important variable for developing a global perspective. Acquiring knowledge about another culture as well as developing the skill to communicate in a language other than one's mother tongue breeds confidence to compete successfully in the global market place. Managing across cultures and national boundaries is difficult and poses complex problems – questions about basic corporate strategy, the quality of expatriate managers staffing the overseas subsidiaries of global enterprises, and the means for developing executives capable of performing successfully in the overseas setting.

Universities represent an important educational resource because of the concentration of international expertise across disciplines. Campus-based education and research and the dissemination of such knowledge are essential contributions of this resource. Within the university setting, schools of business administration should serve as a magnet for the academic, business and professional communities interested and involved in international business. International management should add significantly to the educational progress of students because the field has the unique perspective of adding an international dimension to business and management related courses.

Has research in the field of international management progressed to the point where it can offer scholars and students knowledge about the managing processes worldwide that will enable them to meet their needs? The theme of the University of Windsor's conference,"The Development of a Research Agenda for International Management Research for the 1990's and Beyond" suggests the relative immaturity of the field. Idealistically, one can argue that in the long run international management will be integrated into management research in such a way that international or global management issues and knowledge will be woven throughout existing courses. A global perspective about markets and the management process will be such an integral element in one's orientation that it will become irrelevant to differentiate artificially between domestic and international markets or to ascribe greater importance to the domestic marketplace because it is the location of the corporation's headquarters.

With a field's youth and immaturity comes a sense of inquisitiveness, urgency, lack of direction and non-systematic research. (Everything is fair game.) The present situation is such that no matter how many international management issues researchers study and learn about, there remains a vast unexplored area beckoning researchers and scholars to develop rigorous theory, test hypothesized relationships and venture into the unknown. Although the opportunities to learn more about the practice of international management are virtually limitless, there is a need to help provide more structure and discipline to the field. Even more, scholars must engage in the process of critically reviewing, evaluating, classifying and generalizing about the existing body of substantive research as well as addressing the methodological issues associated with research design and data analysis of research projects.

The Windsor Conference should prove to be a watershed for international management because of its theme, the content of the papers presented at the conference and the conclusions reached by the participants. A review of the papers and summaries presented in this volume are indicative of the resurging vitality and creative thinking associated within the field. The inclusion of representatives from multinational corporations who interacted with the academic representatives added an ingredient unexpected in traditional academic meetings. For established international management researchers as well as management researchers interested in launching internationally grounded research projects, the Windsor conference should be productive because it showcased some of the currently interesting international management issues; and it produced suggested directions for research in the upcoming decade of the nineties. The reader should be stimulated by the new and provocative perspectives that emerged during the sessions. For example, it was suggested that researchers consider explanations other than culture as the basis for differences between results collected in multiple regional settings.

Researchers have come to rely upon culture as the explanatory variable, and in this regard it has become a "garbage can" variable used to explain all regional differences regardless of competing explanations. Organization theorists educated in Western business schools have assumed that organizational success as defined in the West is applicable regardless of the cultural setting. However, is such an assumption valid in terms of our accruing body of international management knowledge and practice? Attendees of the conference questioned the ethnocentric perspective that organization success in one cultural setting was similar to that in another setting. It was concluded that viewing organizational success as a culture free variable is naive in light of the current foment occurring in management scholarship and in management practice. Organization and Human Resource Management theorists should find this volume to be a treasure trove of ideas that impact their respective fields.

As I reflect upon the general state of the international management field, there are at least four fundamental dimensions by which the area should be judged. These variables include theory development, research design and methodology, problematic driven research studies and the role of the international management scholar and researcher. In the remainder of this paper, I will share some of my thoughts on each of these dimensions in the context of international management.

10.1.1 Theory Development

"Data without theory is chaos, and theory without data is a daydream" (Lawler, 1971:37); unfortunately international management has been plagued by both conditions. As a field of study, the rigorous development of international management has suffered because of the lack of theory, inadequate research methodologies to overcome the difficulties of doing high quality, tightly designed research, limited knowledge to interpret the findings of research projects and a small number of well-qualified researchers. However, several of these conditions have been ameliorated within the last several years.

An international management researcher will be remiss if he or she fails to review the relevant behavioral and social science knowledge as they begin to develop a research question, design the project and interpret the data from the project. For example, Cheng has presented several papers concerned with cross-national research and organization-society interactions (Cheng, 1984). In a similar vein, Bhagat and McQuaid(1982) have suggested important and provocative insights about culture and micro-organizational behavior research. These fields can be easily accessed today, and there is little excuse for not tapping into these rich bodies of knowledge. The benefits from the inclusion of such knowledge can only lead to a more significant piece of scholarship.

Serious reviews of international management research have begun to appear in well-established academic journals, and these reviews have been helpful in providing assessments of the field, developing frameworks for classifying the findings of rigorously defined research studies and suggesting directions for future research. Editorial boards of refereed journals have become much more demanding in terms of the requirement for theory-based, cumulative-designed research studies. Special issues of the leading refereed management journals are being devoted to international management research studies and theory development. It is the quality of the articles appearing in these journals, the rigor demanded by editors and their editorial boards that have helped to influence the direction and quality of international management research and publication. The result is that a body of theory is beginning to accrue about strategy, structure and control systems of multinational corporations, as well as models testing hypothesized relationships. The group discussions at the Windsor conference attest to this conclusion.

Although there are large areas of the international management field that remain unexplored, there are several landmark bits of knowledge emerging within the field. To name a few of these areas in which significant progress has taken place, I would include the Human Resource Management subfields of staffing, training and development and management succession, Organization Theory including organization structure and definitions of organization success, Business Policy and Strategic Management incorporating the political impact of strategic alliances and the impact of ideological movements on multinational corporations' strategies. Several of the keynote papers presented at this conference reflect the vibrant growth, in-depth understanding and systematization occurring in the field.

Researchers and scholars are beginning to ask much more sophisticated and thoughtful research-oriented questions, and these queries are more often than not grounded in theory. These conditions bode well for the continuing vitality of the field. However, I would recommend the researcher remain sensitive to two potential challenges: (1) identifying and classifying current multinational corporations' management practices and approaches because the world of affairs has become the laboratory for the academic researcher; and (2) developing appropriate theory and research stemming from fields that have applicability to international management. Failure to heed these challenges can lead to irrelevant, trivial, encapsulated and uninteresting research studies.

10.1.2 Research Design and Methodology

International management research has been plagued by methodological and conceptual problems including such issues as research design, the assumptions underlying the design of the research project and the interpretation of data. It is my opinion that research design and the ensuing methodology have been the Achilles heel for many international management-oriented research studies. The researcher must take special pains to cope with these issues as a research project is formulated. However, researchers should view these problems "not as a weakness but rather as an indication that the field is continuing to grapple with the most important issues" (Adler, 1983, 45).

There are rays of encouragement appearing in management-oriented journals and at professional meetings, and I believe that researchers would be well served to review this literature. Professor David Ricks cites the fall 1983 issue of *Journal of International Business Studies* as an important example of a set of articles addressing the problems of data collection and data analysis. These articles are well worth reading and then re-reading because they are most helpful in the establishment of the foundations for engaging in international management-oriented research projects.

Important criteria the researcher must consider in the design of a research project include the following: (1) a commitment to design studies in which theory plays the central role for the genesis of the study and interpretation of the results; (2) attention to the accepted practices and procedures for testing hypothesized relationships, and the commitment to design and carry out rigorous research studies. The place of anecdotal research has become less and less a characteristic of international management research and publication; and (3) an understanding of the importance and commitment to build upon or extend the existing body of management knowledge. Cumulative rather than disorganized and random research studies must become the hallmark of international management research. These factors, among others, will contribute significantly to the rigor of the study and its ultimate contribution to the body of knowledge and the development of the field.

10.1.3 Problem Driven Research

International management researchers and, consequently, the field have much to gain by interacting with executives and managers engaged in international business. The field requires the constant infusion of new ideas and approaches from those firms who are competing with others in the international marketplace. The impact of regional forces upon corporate strategy development, models of organization structure, communication and control mechanisms, management styles and human resource management practices are among some of the day-to-day issues and problems that multinational corporations have to cope with. These real-life experiences present a rich vein of practical knowledge and insight that must be transferred to international management researchers and scholars, and ultimately into educational course materials designed for students preparing for careers in business as well as present managers participating in executive and management development programs.

The corporation competing in the global marketplace is the laboratory for testing new models, developing new techniques for successfully coping with the intense competition and becoming sensitive to the management problems. At this point in time, researchers must come to accept the notion that much of the advancement of thinking and practice in the international areas may flow from the corporate setting rather than academe. In other words, we as academics will be the learners and collaborators with management rather than the teachers. By means of continual interchange with the multinational corporation, researchers will be working on problem-driven research issues, reflecting on what they had found in their research projects, encouraged to publish their findings in refereed journals and striving to advance theory and construct models.

The field of international management is composed of two hemispheres, one theoretic and the other applied, and if international management, as a field, is to grow and develop, there must be an ongoing interaction between the two. Guaranteeing a vigorous and vital relationship depends on the academic researcher who is comfortable and familiar with activities occurring in both hemispheres. Corporations and their management have been challenged to devise the mechanisms for coping with the rapidly changing conditions of the highly competitive worldwide economic environment in which they exist. Management frequently has little or no time to reflect upon theoretical explanations and solutions to their problems. Management must respond in ways which work best for them, and there is likely to be little attention given to an elaborate theoretical explanation that offers little or no chance of application. This is not to be construed as a call to disregard theoretical research because it is not. The researcher can bring his or her theoretical training to bear on real problems; and, in turn, practical experience can help to enrich theory development, model building and future research agenda.

10.2 The Role of the Academic Researcher in the Field of International Management

There are more and more demands being factored into the role of the academic researcher, and the problem becomes that of trying to reconcile the various demands. Throughout this article, attention has been given to the importance of the corporation's potential contributions to an enriched and relevant field of international management. However, how does the researcher and ultimately the field become aware of the economic, social and managerial problems facing the multinational corporation? Who plays the role of identifier, classifier and critic of the corporations' response to the economic, social and managerial problems it faces? It should be the international management researcher and scholar who plays the nexus between theory and practice.

What are some of the steps that the academic researcher may exercise in order to bridge the gap between his or her theoretical, academic training and the practical demands of managers of multinational corporations? There are multiple dimensions to the academic researcher's role. First, international management researchers can learn a great deal by becoming familiar with the current management practices of those firms doing international business. What does this entail? It means that the academic researcher must be sensitive to larger organizational, social, legal and economic issues associated with the management of firms engaged in doing international business, and more specifically it requires the researcher to become familiar with the organizational problems confronting management.

Second, when an academic researcher is engaged in a company-supported research project, it is important that the researcher come up with suggestions and viable propositions that can be implemented. It is difficult to justify an academic researcher who is limited to providing theoretical, and perhaps unrealistic or impractical solutions to real problems. This is not to imply that company-supported research projects have no place in the contribution to theory development because that is not true. Ideally one is seeking a blend of the two.

Third, the academic researcher, whose advice is sought by representatives of multinational firms, must develop his or her problem-solving skills. This will require that the researcher develop a broad range understanding of techniques and their applicability to the organizational problems at hand. The academic may not know the ultimate solution to the industrial problem at hand, but he or she can identify the problem, specify its parameters and suggest a variety of workable technical applications to the problem. Perhaps this is one of the more distinct changes occurring in the role of the academic researcher because in this regard the researcher has learned what has worked in the business world and what has not.

Fourth, the academic researcher has an important role as an educator responsible for helping to prepare tomorrow's cadre of managers as well as current managers engaged in the management of the firm in international competition. The researcher and scholar capable of blending theoretical and practical knowledge and understanding is the best of the two worlds, and he or she can contribute significantly to the international research agenda of the 1990's.

10.3 Conclusion

International management is a field in transition, and as a developing field it has been plagued by many of the shortcomings associated with an emerging field including: (1) a disregard for attending to conceptual and methodological-oriented research paradigms; (2) researchers who fail to build upon the existing body of knowledge or who disregard the potential contributions of other fields of management or internationally related scholarship; and (3) the publication of research findings that has little relevance to the development of theory or the day-to-day practice of management. Today those criticisms are being blunted because the field has evolved toward a commitment to theory development, rigorously designed research studies and a process of cumulative research. The "right questions are being asked, and that is as it should be. In contrast the right technology to answer some of those questions is yet to be developed" (Adler, 1983, 45). Overall, I take these signs to be positive, and we should take some measure of enthusiasm over the vigor and vitality of the field in comparison to 10 years ago. However, I admonish the researcher not to become complacent with the progress that has occurred in the last five to eight years.

International management is in a transitional state and the progress of the field and its relevance to management practice will depend upon the researcher's skill, ability and commitment to excellent scholarship and research. Throughout this article I have sketched an outline of the challenges, pressures and demands confronting the field in general and the researcher in particular. If international management is to make a contribution to the education of current and future managerial personnel, it will be the scholar and researcher who will play an instrumental role in the educational process. This conference was indicative of the scholar, researcher and manager foment occurring in the field: solid conceptual thinking, identification of emerging trends, willingness to challenge assumptions, spirited discussions and the inclusion of an industrial perspective combined in such a way as to augur well for the future of the field.

Finally, I challenge the field to begin to think globally about itself. International management is not limited to a Western, much less a North American, definition of the management process. Collaborative research across disciplines and across cultures should be an item of high priority. Those of us educated in North America have much to learn about management as seen through others' eyes. We don't have a monopoly on creative management thought and effective, efficient management practice.

These are exciting times, and researchers have an opportunity to help change the direction of the field, integrating the field into management theory and practice, exploring new areas and enriching management practice. Given the nature of the global economic competition, international management has an important role to play.

10.4 References

Adler, N J. (1983). A Typology of Management Studies Involving Culture, *Journal of International Business Studies,* 14, 2, 29–47.

Bhagat, R. and S.McQuaid (1982). Role of Subjective Culture in Organizations: A Review and Directions for Future Research. *Journal of Applied Psychology,* 67, 653–685.

Cheng, J. (1984). The Role of Cross-national Research in Organizational Inquiry: A Review and Proposal. *Academy of Management Proceedings 1984,* Columbia, S.C.: Academy of Management, 90–94.

Journal of International Business Studies, 14, 2 (Fall, 1983).

Kobrin, S., (1984). *International Expertise in American Business.* New York: Institute of International Education.

Lawler, E.E. (1971). *Pay and Organizational Effectiveness: A Psychological View,* New York: McGraw-Hill.

Tung, R.L. (1988). *The New Expatriates: Managing Human Resources Abroad.* Cambridge, MA: Ballinger Publishers.

11 Research for International Management – Practitioners' Perspectives

W. A. Pursell
London Consulting Group
R. J. Radway
Radway and Associates U.S.A.

11.1 Introduction: A Practitioner's View of Academic Research

It is clear to us that international management is here to stay. The days of the pure local or home country manager are numbered. In the business and political world which is evolving, no manager is free from the impact of international competition, direct of indirect. We feel, therefore, that it is essential to re-examine, from time to time, the relevance and effectiveness of university and business school international management research.

We should state at the outset that we, as practitioners, are not necessarily looking for perfection. We do not believe that perfection in international management is any more real, or relevant, than is perfection in competition. In the dynamic and uneven world of business, what may seem perfect in one situation could be much less so in another.

Perhaps the key is to look for constant improvement in international management methods and practices. Competition, in our view, demands that management does not remain static and that improvements show in a tangible way in the marketplace, in the production unit, or in the use of resources. What is unfortunate is that, in the hurly-burly of day-to-day competition, business management has little time, and perhaps little inclination, to develop new approaches and practices for success in international business.

This is where academia and the intermediary business consultants come into play. To coin a phrase, it would appear that there is a triad of interests which should be working together to advance the further development of international management effectiveness. In the simplest terms, we see academics as the thinkers and researcher who form new ideas, the consulting fraternity as the current interpreters and communicators of such ideas, and business and government as the relevant customers.

This is where we, as customer and consulting practitioner respectively, begin to have some problems. It is our view that not enough attention is normally given to identifying the needs of the customers themselves in industry and in government. Perhaps of equal importance, it would appear that the effectiveness of academia's communication of new ideas to the potential users, in useable form, leaves much to be desired.

As a general observation it is our view that, with a few exceptions, researchers in academia tend to focus on academia itself as the relevant customer. This view was corroborated, and indeed sharpened, by attendance at the Annual Meeting of the Academy of International Business in San Diego in October, 1988. The over-riding impression was one of academia talking at, and sometimes past, itself. The reasons for this are, we think, fairly evident and understandable: a drive for higher academic qualifications among experienced researcher, and perhaps the desire for accolades and prestige among the higher levels of academia. These are all very worthwhile in their own right, but are not necessarily consistent with the particular needs of the international business community.

11.2 The Roles of the University in International Management

To get a possible answer, we believe that it is useful to step back and try to describe the various roles which should be filled by academia, from the point of practitioners in international business. We see these roles as:

1. the educating, training and preparation of a constant flow of graduates for business and government;

2. the continuous re-education of business people in proven concepts and approaches as they evolve;

3. the provision of research assistance to help solve specific problems in international business as they arise;

4. the anticipation and evaluation of future change, and assistance in grasping the opportunities of solving the problems expected to arise; and

5. the development of an effective two-way communication with the business/government community itself on needs and solutions.

With respect to the flow of graduates, we do not have the temerity to suggest change in this role. We can visualize, however, the added benefit which could accrue to potential graduates from regular exposure to practitioners from business, government and the consulting fraternity. Some academic institutions are, of course, already pursuing such an activity of academia to persuade senior management of companies and government that this would ultimately benefit them.

It would appear that the role of re-educating business people is perhaps one of the stronger areas of activity for many universities and business schools. This occurs normally through conferences, seminars, formal courses, and an overwhelming flow of printed matter. The problem is that, for the average businessman, most of the printed matter is not in useable form and he depends upon consultants to analyze this matter and interpret it for his specific needs.

11.3 The Need for Closer Links to Consultancy and Practice

We believe that two actions would be helpful here: first, that academic researchers work more closely with business consultants and, second, that members of academia try to link themselves more directly to the potential end-user of their research efforts. We will deal with these thoughts more fully in subsequents comments.

The core of the issue at hand arises from the next two roles noted above, namely, research to solve existing problems and research to anticipate and prepare for future problems and opportunities. In a sense, we see academia as a research laboratory for companies and for government. Having said that, we would point out that successful research of any kind most frequently arises from being tied-in closely to the marketplace and to the ultimate customer.

International business research is no exception and yet we are terribly conscious of a reluctance in academia to take the somewhat impure step of contacting business directly. There seems to be an apprehension that dealing directly with the ultimate customer will somehow tarnish the image and objectivity of academia. Many institutions seem to prefer the purity of isolation although it makes increasingly less sense as the global economy evolves.

In contrast, we would draw attention to the activities of organizations such as the American Management Association (AMA) and Business International Corporation (BI). They deliberately seek out the current and

future issues of concern to international management by use of industry
advisory committees, management councils, round tables, executive conferences, and sponsored research programs directed at industry management. A relevant question in a very recent AMA survey was:

> In your experience, what are the most serious problems that companies must
> face in doing business abroad (e.g., researching potential markets, choosing
> joint-venture partners overseas, hiring local managers, repatriating profits,
> etc.)?

Is there any reason for individual academic institutions not to have advisory committees and councils drawn form international business and to
sponsor surveys to establish business needs and concerns on a global
basis? Why not also use the business consulting industry, as they do, to
get input for business and to interpret output from academic research for
industry.?

A further example of an AMA question to one of its advisory committees in May, 1988 read as follows:

> In strategic management, what are some global needs and issues that the
> AMA should be addressing (e.g., multinational linkages)? How can we best
> explore and approach these needs and issues?

An example of one reply to this question is attached as Appendix 1. We
believe that this kind of communication from business could be a valuable
tool for academia to use in determining relevant research projects in international business management.

11.4 Implications

This brings us logically to the final role which we see as appropriate for
academia, namely, effective communication of international business research needs and results. As implied in several places above, we believe
that this role is the one filled least successfully by academia. We have
several suggestions to offer for consideration:

1. as Henry Mintzberg suggested, go and interview managers for
   feedback;
2. arrange for researchers to sit with managers and see the complica-
   tions and constraints in real-life situations;
3. offer knowledgeable researchers as facilitators for individual company task-forces on issues (e.g., strategy for the European Community post-1992);

4. use available consultants for networking throughout international business;

5. persuade companies to accept a research professor as a mentor on international business issues and develop a "buddy system" where there is an ongoing two-way flow and benefit;

6. bring an executive-in-residence into the business faculty for up to one year (but has to be anchored at the CEO level to facilitate executive re-entry and interim financing); develop "real world" networks for each academic institution and submit case studies, articles, research papers or proposals, etc. for comment before publishing.

As a final point, we appreciate that the eternal underlying issue for academia is financing, for business research or any other like activity. The universities and business schools have a job to do; they must persuade international business companies, governments at various levels, private foundations, and other financial sources, that their research will be relevant, effectively communicated, timely, and cost-effective.

This is not an easy job, nor is it one that many members of academia will find particularly comfortable. But we feel deeply that, unless academia is prepared to sell itself and its research output to interested buyers, the relevance and usefulness of its work will be of increasingly limited value to the international business community.

11.5 Appendix 1: Response to AMA letter May 25, 1988

Question:

> In strategic management, what are some global needs and issues that the AMA should be addressing (e.g., multinational linkages)? How can we best explore and approach these needs and issues?

Response:

1. Free or freer trade within major geographic blocs, and perhaps between blocs, is becoming a reality. What should North American businesses, both smaller local and major international, be doing to prepare for this development? What should AMA be doing to help various-sized companies to compete effectively?

2. With leading-edge companies likely to become increasingly international in investment (and therefore organization), what steps

should be taken to prepare North American management to manage far-flung subsidiaries and, probably, managers from other cultures? Can AMA help, perhaps in concert with comparable European and/or- (APAC) institutions including universities?

3. Individual company competitive advantages: what should North American companies be seeking to do which, in world markets, will provide the best chance of advantage over both European and APAC companies for common consumers? AMA could examine what particular elements in the competitive chain are used by successful companies in each region and communicate these approaches in its programs.

4. Should the AMA *itself* be changing so that it is recognized as the International Management Association, rather that the American Management Association? Should it organize itself differently and consciously move towards more multi-national, multi-cultural personnel and locations?

5. With the increasing globalization of companies (regardless of national origin), the issue of business/government relations is emerging as being of critical importance. North American companies will have to learn how to deal effectively with this issue, often in different cultures. Could the AMA take a lead here by incorporating the different elements of this issue in its strategic management teaching and suggest how business might approach the various problems which could arise?

6. There is likely to be increasing incidence of joint-venture companies and strategic alliances in one form or another. Perhaps AMA can explore the various forms that such cooperations can take, including the pros and cons of each one so that the business manager will be better able to assess the approach most suitable for his particular situation.

12 Strategies for Achieving Relevance

Durhane Wong-Rieger
University of Windsor
Fritz Rieger
University of Windsor

12.1 Introduction

This chapter discusses the principal findings from the conference and the survey and suggest some overall strategies for achieving relevance in International Management research. Basically, four types of prescriptions for change were indicated: (1) change what we study; (2) change our conceptual frameworks; (3) change how we study; and (4) change with whom and for whom we study.

12.1.1 Change What We Study

Changing the content of International management research is based on the premise that the current lack of relevance is due to examining the wrong issues. In the words of Thomas and Tymon (1982), there is a lack of goal relevance in that the dependent variables of the researcher are not transferable to the goals of the manager in the field. Prior to the conference, Ricks (1988) had polled selected members of the international management division of the Academy of Management regarding their suggestions for future research projects. In general, he found that most of these could be classified into the traditional areas, including strategic management, human resources management, organizational behavior and cross-national management, organization and control and production. Perhaps the most important new issue identified from both this survey and conference was the need to move beyond the levels of the organization and the individual to examine relationships between different levels and between the organization and the environment. One suggestion was to link the domestic operations and the international strategies of a firm with the

broader economic, political and social environments in which they operate. The second need was to consider the influence of both home and host
governments, especially as host governments take an increasingly active
role toward regulating or controlling foreign-based organizations. In this
regard, a specific issue was to examine how the amount of power exerted
by the host government on foreign businesses affected the relationship
between transnational alliance partners. Another possible topic was the
ability of states to handle transnational legal issues, such as the Bohpal
incident. A third focus of domestic-international research of considerable
practical importance was the process of "backyard globalization" and its
implications. For example, what is the impact of foreign competition on
firms operating strictly in a domestic market? What strategies should affected industries or firms adopt in order to be proactive rather than reactive in their dealings with foreign entries?

12.1.2 Change the Conceptual Frameworks

A second change to increase relevance is a change in the conceptual
frameworks used to conduct IM research. One criticism of the current
models of transnational partnerships was that they were incomplete and
biased and derived primarily from studies of Western-based organizations.
As noted, most of the research to date has taken place with North American multinational corporations and ignored other forms of alliances, in
particular, more cooperative transnational coalitions such as joint ventures, licensing arrangements, and franchises. Moreover, these models do
not take into consideration the previously mentioned environmental factors such as political instability, host government power, and the influence
of other major stakeholders (such as kinship ties in the Chinese organizational system [Redding, 1988]). Because these factors play a lesser role
in the operation of the MNC, it is important to study partnerships in other
contexts.

The goal would be to develop a typology of organizational relationships
which would take into consideration the various forms of organizational
structures and relationships. Such a typology should have relevance to
both theory and practice. From the conference, ten dimensions comprising
three categories were suggested for defining this typology. These were
broad environmental conditions (Host/Home Government Influence, Political Stability, Local Politics, and Local Culture), relational dimensions

(Stage of Partnership, Formal Coordination among Partners, Relative Power of Partners, and Time Frame for Alliance), and organization-specific dimensions (Level of internationalization of the organization; Level of internationalization of the work-force).

These were subsequently presented to the 50 participants, who were asked to rate them in terms of their importance in defining a research typology. Responses were received from 60% of the group. Overall, all of the dimensions were rated fairly closely in importance, indicating a high level of consensus but also a fairly complex conceptual framework. The two dimensions rated as most important were the Level of Internationalization of the Organization and Host/Home Government Influence. The second set were the Local Culture and the Relative Power of the Partners, which was followed by Local Politics.

In combining these recommendations, we propose a four-dimensional model for conducting IM research. The first dimension consists of all the environmental conditions under which the transnational alliance takes place. These include the government influences, culture, politics and economic situations of the two (or more) partners. We hesitate to label these conditions as variables, since it is unlikely that they operate independently. Rather, they would interact to define an over-arching set of environmental conditions which, depending on the goals of the researcher and organization, might be defined by terms such as favourable, risky, or stable.

The second dimension focuses on organizational-level factors. These include, among other things, the form of international activity in which the firm is engaged, the level of international experience, the extent of global activities, and the importance of international operations to the overall strategy of the firm. Again, these internal characteristics would coalesce to define the potential competence of the firm as an actor in the international market. A newer dimension is that which encompasses the relational elements of the cross-national partnership. Thus, the relative power of the respective members, the degree of formal or informal coordination required, and the stage to which the partnership has evolved all need to be considered in defining the overall quality of the alliance and how the partners are likely to behave toward each other. Quite obviously, this dimension is influenced considerably by the first two. Thus, when the overall environments are less stable, it may be necessary for the foreign-based company to entail more formal coordination mechanisms than when it is dealing in a country which has highly favorable political and economic conditions. Likewise, an organization which is entering a partnership where the other firm has considerably more international experience, might be alert to the potential imbalance in power and prepare itself by taking appropriate measures in the prearrangements.

There is likely a high degree of mutual influence among all three dimensions, so that the nature of the relationships may also influence the environment dimension. Thus, a large multinational or stateless enterprise, as described by Kobrin (1988) could excite a host government to invoke more controls in an attempt to constrain the impact on the country. Conversely, and equally likely, the weaker government could be persuaded not to interfere, for fear of the loss of the economic benefits contributed by the powerful MNC.

Finally, the framework proposes the inclusion of a time dimension to pick up the dynamic nature of the practice-oriented research process. That research is understood as a process, and an interactive one, is critical. As discussed by Pettigrew (1985), research in this arena is characterized in the language of muddling through, incrementalism, and political process rather than as rational, foresightful, goal-directed activity. He notes that while we tend to acknowledge this as true in the organizations which we study, we continue to think of our own research as exercises in technical rationality.

Unfortunately, this is the one dimension which appears to be least well incorporated into the IM research. Not only was the time-frame for study rated as least important by the respondents in our conference, but, as discussed in the following sections, there was little appreciation for longitudinal research and interaction with the organization.

Overall, the four dimensions could serve as a framework for discovering, interpreting, and testing problems as well as proposing solutions for implementation. It would provide a means for comparing different situations and the results from different research studies. In general, we prefer to use these as dimensions as qualitative rather than as quantitative guides. They should not be rigidly defined by ratings along variables but serve as an imprecise, flexible model for examining problems and the contexts in which they need to be resolved.

12.1.3 Change How We Study

The changes in how to study reiterated much of what has been suggested elsewhere to increase relevance in organizational research. Argyris

(1983), for example, has emphasized the need to depart from interview techniques, which reveal only what the respondent can verbalize (espoused theory) and to engage more actively (through observation and other analytic techniques) to uncover the underlying theories in action. The former, he suggests, results in a lower level of knowing than the latter. According to Hackman (1985) lab methods are very impractical in that they factor out the important contextual variables and even field research methods tend to result in a "static" picture which is unrepresentative of most organizations. At the conference, participants suggested using more of the following: case studies, longitudinal studies, historical case studies, metaphors and analogies, observational field studies of managers, interviews of top management, and academic-practitioner partnerships.

Specific to the field of IM, there has been a call to de-emphasize simple comparative studies, which don't tell much. Rather, there is a move toward more complex designs such as: multicultural, multi-industry samples; multi-level, multi-constituency surveys; multicultural, systematic surveys of practices; studies of cross-cultural mergers; emic field studies of non-Western organizations; and the tracking of career paths of international managers. The methods suggested here attest to the complexity envisioned for conducting meaningful research across constituents differing in culture, politics, and geographic location.

One of the concerns of the survey was to discover whether the academics attending the conference were themselves planning to incorporate more "relevant" approaches in their research strategies. To this effect, they were asked to indicate which methodologies they were currently using and which they planned to use in the near future. The results indicated that the most popular current methodology, by far, was the interview, used by 75% of the group. Case studies were conducted by 54%. Over one-third engaged in longitudinal studies, multicultural surveys, and some form of multicultural-multilevel approach. Most pertinent to the purposes here, however, was the finding that only about one-fifth reported they were currently doing collaborative research with practitioners.

Increases in all of these methodologies were planned for the future. According to their responses, people planned to do more research involving multiple levels within the organizations and across industries and cultural groups. A greater use of multicultural surveys was also anticipated, as well as observations of the international manager in the field. Moreover, a slight decrease in reliance on interviewing was expected, dropping this technique to the second most frequently cited approach. Respondents planned to do more case studies, raising this methodology to first in popularity . What appears somewhat disturbing is the anticipated decline in longitudinal studies. Thus, despite the agreed-upon need for research involving organizations over time and the cautions issued against static research designs, researchers were not planning to follow this advice. Moreover, while more respondents indicated they will be entering practitioner partnerships, the total percentage was still modest (less than one third).

12.1.4   Change With Whom and For Whom We Study

This leads directly, then to the fourth area of change required to achieve relevance: our research partners and clients. It is in this area which we feel IM research needs to do the most "catching up" relative to other organizational fields. In examining the research projects compiled by Cheng (1987) and Rieger and Wong-Rieger (1991) from the members of the International Management division, those received by Ricks prior to the Research for Relevance Conference, and the suggestions expressed at that conference, almost no mention was made of methodologies which involved organizational problem-solving. There are many strategies of this type which could be extended to the IM field. For example, Mitroff and Killman (1983) have proposed a model of "useful scientific inquiry" which begins with identification of a real-world problem, followed by a conceptualization of the phenomenon, and then by the formulation of a scientific model, or theory. From the theory, various implications for the real-world setting are derived; these are tried out in the problem situation, and outcomes evaluated. This leads to either change or reinforcement of the conceptualization. Similarly, Lewin's (1946) action research model involves an iterative process involving fact finding, planning, executing an action step, data gathering to evaluate the action, and planning based on the learnings.

Thomas and Tymon (1982) likewise envisioned a two-way interaction between the researcher and the practitioner, whereby the researcher produced knowledge and the practitioner used it. Another strategy with practical significance which would lend itself well to the IM field is organization design (Litterer and Jelinek, 1983). Finally, survey feedback (Likert, 1961) is another possible borrowing form the organization development field. All of these strategies indicate a much closer relationship between research and useful knowledge than suggested by the prevalent IM research methods.

12.2 Serving Two Masters: Can IM Research be Theoretical and Problem Oriented?

In summary, we have proposed four changes which need to be made to insure that IM research will have relevance, both for academics in their theoretical conceptualizations and understandings and for practitioners in carrying out their strategies and operations more effectively and competitively. The changes of the first type, what the researcher studies, should be derived from the problems experienced by the manager in the real world. This means that the researcher will need to be more involved with the practitioner and his/her real situations in order to discover these problems.

In setting forth the second change, a four-dimensional typology or framework for locating IM studies was proposed. In so doing, the purpose was not to define more precisely the independent and dependent variables for conducting research; rather borrowing form Pettigrew (1985), it was to suggest a context from which one could discover and understand, in a situationally located, holistic fashion, the processes of transnational partnerships and their evolution over time and circumstances. Ideally, the model allows for examination of mutual concerns relevant to the researcher and to the practitioner.

The third area of change, methodology, builds upon much of what IM research already does well, and that is research in field situations using real organizations. There has already been a move away from simple comparative studies; also, what we have not stressed here, because it has been done elsewhere, is the awareness of theory-driven research. Studies which are based on conceptual models, be they inductive or deductive, are critical to the development of findings which move beyond the trivial or the obvious.

The final change is perhaps most crucial and least likely within the established tradition of research in the academic institutions. Basically, we have called for increases in collaborative relationships with practitioners and for conducting research with the client in mind. In conclusion, we would repeat some of the recommendations set forth by Seashore (1983), for business schools, in general, to foster the link between researchers and practitioners. Some of these have already been picked up by the IM field; others may be longer in coming. His first recommendation is to continue to do theoretical, non-site specific research, which is necessary for some purposes. Second, conduct more longitudinal and historical studies. Third, engage in more joint sharing of consulting, like the clinical case review model which draws in experts from various discipline to problem solve a case. Fourth, build in a skills component to the training of graduates. Fifth, codify a set of norms for reporting and disseminating information to various stakeholders. Sixth, modify the training institutions to include supervised internships, to make less demand for publications from new Ph.D's in order that they can acquire the necessary field experience, and to provide publication outlets for "practical" articles. We would add to this step the development of forms for sharing of research results with consultants and managers. Finally, he stresses the use of interdisciplinary teams, a methodological recommendation which may be highly valid in as complex a field as IM.

12.3 References

Argyris, C. (1983). Usable Knowledge for Double-loop Problems. In R.H. Kilmann, K.W. Thomas, D.P. Slevin, R. Nath, and S.L. Jerrell (eds.) *Producing Useful Knowledge for Organizations*. New York: Praeger. 377–394.

Cheng, J. (1987) International and Comparative Management Research Directory. 5th Ed. Report for International Management Division, Academy of Management.

Hackman, J.R. (1985) Doing Research that Makes a Difference. In E.E. Lawler III, A.M. Mohrman Jr., A.A. Mohrman, G.E. Ledford Jr., and T.G. Cummings (eds.) *Doing Research that is Useful for Theory and Practice*. San Francisco: Jossey-Bass. 126–148.

Kobrin, S.(1988). Global Firms and Nation States. Paper presented at conference on Research for Relevance in International Management, University of Windsor, Ontario.

Lewin, K. (1946). Action Research and Minority Problems. *Journal of Social Issues,* 2, 34–46.

Likert, R. (1961). *New patterns of management.* New York: McGraw-Hill.

Litterer, J.A. and M. Jelinek (1983). Design as a Setting for Future Research. In R.H. Kilmann, K.W. Thomas, D.P. Slevin, R. Nath, and S.L. Jerrell (eds.) *Producing Useful Knowledge for Organizations.* New York: Prager, 454–467.

Mitroff, I. I. and R.H. Kilmann (1983). Intellectual Resistance to Useful Knowledge: An Archetypal Social Analysis. In R.H. Kilmann, K.W. Thomas, D.P. Slevin, R. Nath, and S.L. Jerrell (eds.) *Producing Useful Knowledge for Organizations.* New York: Prager, 266–280.

Pettigrew, A. M. (1985). Contextualist Research: A Natural Way to Link Theory and Practice. In E.E. Lawler III, A.M. Mohrman Jr., A.A. Mohrman, G.E. Ledford Jr., and T.G. Cummings (eds.) *Doing Research that is Useful for Theory and Practice.* San Francisco: Jossey-Bass, 79–106.

Pursell, W. (1988). Relevant Research for International Managers: A Practitioners View. Paper presented at Annual Conference of the Academy of International Business, San Diego, California.

Redding, S. G. (1988). Beyond Bureaucracy: Towards a Comparative Analysis of Forms of Economic Resource Coordination and Control. Paper presented at Conference on Research for Relevance in International Management. University of Windsor, Ontario.

Ricks, D. (1988). Research Topics in International Management. Paper presented at Conference on Research for Relevance in International Management. University of Windsor, Ontario.

Rieger, F. and D. Wong-Rieger, (1991). *International Management Research Directory,* 6th edition. Windsor, Ontario: Academy of Management.

Seashore, S. E. (1983). Organizational Change. In S.E. Seashore, E.E. Lawler II, P.H. Mirvis and C. Cammann (eds.) *Assessing Organizational Change.* New York: John Wiley and Sons, 1–13.

Thomas, K. W. and W. G. Tymon Jr. (1982). Necessary Properties of Relevant Research: Lessons From Recent Criticisms of the Organizational Sciences. *Academy of Management Review,* 7, 345–352.

Author biographies

Nancy J. Adler is Professor of Organizational Behavior at McGill University in Montreal where she twice received the Distinguished Teaching Award in Management. Dr Adler conducts research and consults on strategic international human resource management, expatriation, women in international management, and international organization development. She has authored numerous articles, produced the film, *A portable Life,* and published the books, *International Dimensions of Organizational Behavior* and *Women in Management Worldwide*. Dr. Adler has consulted on projects throughout the world and has taught in Hong Kong, China, France and Italy. She was selected a 3M Teaching Fellow (1991) and was elected a Fellow of the Academy of International Business (1992).

Fariborz Ghadar is Professor and Chairman of the International Business Department at The George Washington University School of Business and Public Management. He specializes in international finance and banking, corporate strategy and global economic assessment. Dr. Ghadar is also chairman of the Intrados/International Management Group, a Washington-based consortium of experts in international business. He has served as a consultant to a score of major corporations and governments. Before jointing the George Washington University, Dr. Ghadar was president of the Export Promotion Center for the government of Iran. He has published four books and is also the publisher of SWAPS: The Newsletter of new Financial Instruments.

Stephen J. Kobrin is William H. Wurster Professor Multinational Management at the Wharton School where he teaches international business and international political-economy. His research interests include political risk, international strategic management, global integration and the interaction of international business and international politics. Professor Kobrin is a Fellow of the Academy of International Business and has served as Chair of the Eastern Region and of the Dissertation Award Committee. He was Book Review Editor of the *Journal of International Business Studies* (JIBS) and is currently on the editorial boards of *JIBS*, *The Academy of Management Journal* and *International Organization*.

Edwin L. Miller is Associate Dean for Research and Professor at the Michigan Business School, The University of Michigan. He received his

Ph.D. degree from the University of California, Berkeley, and he joined the Michigan faculty in 1964.

Professor Miller has held leadership positions in a variety of professional societies, and was elected a Fellow in the Academy of Management in 1984. He has published more than 40 articles on comparative and international management and personnel/human resource management in refereed journals. His current research interests are in management development and succession planning among multinational corporations.

Henry Mintzberg is Professor of Management at McGill University in Montreal where he does his research and writing on the process of strategy formation, the design of organizations, and the roles of intuition, insight and inspiration in a world of "thin" management. He received his doctorate from the MIT Sloan School of Management and has been granted honorary degrees from the Universities of Venice, Lund and Laussane. From 1988 to 1991 he served as President of the Strategic Management Society, a worldwide association of "thoughtful practitioners and insightful scholars." He is a Fellow of the Royal Society of Canada (the first elected from a management faculty), the Academy of Management, and the International Academy of Management. Dr. Mintzberg is the author of five books and over seventy articles and has recently completed a book about "the rise and fall of strategic planning."

Richard B. Peterson is Professor of Management and Organization in the School of Business Administration at the University of Washington. His current research interests include Japanese management, international industrial relations and human resources management, grievance processes, and problem-solving bargaining. He is a former Chair of the International Management Division of the Academy of Management. He is editing a forthcoming book on managers in 15 different countries that includes the role of culture on managerial behavior and how managers are impacted by human resource management activities.

Betty Jane Punnett is a native of St. Vincent and the Grenadines, and has lived and worked in the Caribbean and the U.S. Currently she is Associate Professor of at the University of Windsor in Canada, where she teaches international business and management. She recently published International Business with D. Ricks and is completing International Management with D. Ricks and M. Mendenhall. Past research, covering the Far East, the Caribbean and North America has appeared in a wide variety of journals. She is currently editing (with O. Shenkar) an issue of International Studies of Management and Organization focussing on doing research in less familiar locations.

Mr. William Pursell obtained his M.A. in economics at the University of Glasgow in 1951 and moved to Canada where he held marketing and economic forecasting positions with Dunlop Canada and Cortaulds North America. He joined Polysar Ltd as an economic associate and subsequently rose to positions of Sales Director North and South America for twelve years and then directed corporate strategic activity and global strategic planning for the polymers side of the company. Following early retirement in 1990, he was appointed Senior Research Fellow of the National Center for Management Research and Development at the Western business School. He consults on Strategic Planning through the London Consulting Group.

Robert J. Radway is Managing Director of Vector International, a New York based strategic management consulting firm for companies interested in improving strategy implementation abroad. Since 1988 he has also taught short courses at leading Business Schools in Europe, and since 1976 executive programs in Europe, Asia and North and South America. His main interests are globalization of the firm, alliances and joint ventures, mergers and acquisitions and the role of the global manager. He has 30 years practical experience in international business, has published extensively in legal and practitioner's publications, and is listed in *Who's Who in America and other Who's Whos.*

Gordon Redding holds the Chair of Management Studies and is Director of the University of Hong Kong Business School and the Poon Kam Kai Institute of Management. He has devoted nearly two decades to research on cross-cultural aspects of management in Pacific Asia, specializing in the overseas Chinese. This has resulted in approximately 90 articles and four books. He is on the editorial boards of a variety of journals and is a member of many professional and business organizations in Asia. His current research is in three fields: the comparison of business cultures in Pacific Asia; the implications of the Overseas Chinese for China; and the cross-cultural operating problems of multinationals.

Fritz Rieger is Associate Professor of Management at the University of Windsor where he researches how societal culture affects organizational learning in international joint ventures. He has been generally interested in how culture affects organizations and his doctoral research, which focussed on cultural influences in the international airline industry, received the Richard Farmer award of the Academy of International Business for best dissertation in 1987. He was co-editor of the Academy of Management International Management Division Research Directory for 1991. He was visiting professor of management at the Lyon Graduate School of Business in France in 1992.

Dr. David A. Ricks is Vice President for Academic Affairs at Thunderbird – The American Graduate School of International Management. Dr. Ricks has written nine books including most recently *International Business: An Introduction* and *Blunders in International Business*. He is also the author of scores of articles and papers. Besides having served as the Editor-in-Chief of the *Journal of International Business Studies* for the past eight years, Dr. Ricks is a member of the editorial board for eight journals, including the *Journal of Business Research*. He has served as chair of the International Division of the Academy of Management and as the Treasurer of the Academy of International Business.

Alan M. Rugman is Professor of International Business at the University of Toronto. As a leading authority on international business, professor Rugman served as Vice President of the Academy of International Business in 1989–1990 and was elected a Fellow of the Academy in 1991. He has lectured widely across North America, in Western Europe and in East Asia. He has published over 100 articles and 16 books dealing with the economic, managerial, and strategic aspects of multinational enterprises and with trade and investment policy. He has been selected for inclusion in the *Canadian Who's Who* and *Who's Who in the World*.

Rosalie L. Tung is Professor Business Administration and first holder of the Ming and Stella Wong Chaired Professorship in International Business, Simon Fraser University She was formerly a Wisconsin Distinguished professor, Business Administration, with the University of Wisconsin System. She is the author of seven books and has also published widely on the subjects of international management and organizational theory in the leading journals in the fields of international business, management and human resources. Professor Tung has served on the Board of Governors of the Academy of Management and the Executive Board of the Academy of International Business. She is active in the internationalization of business schools worldwide.

Durhane Wong-Rieger is Associate Professor of Psychology and director of the Human Resources Consultation Unit at the University of Windsor. Her research interests have included the adaptation of immigrants and sojourners to living abroad, acculturation issues in international joint ventures, and organizational evaluation in health and human services organizations. Dr. Wong-Rieger has published articles on research methodology, psychology of group membership, cultural adapatation, international management and strategic decision making She consults widely in both the public and private sector and is a member of the Excutive Board of the Canadian Hemophilia Society. She is also chair of the Industrial and Organizational Psychology division of the Canadian Psychological Association.

Subject Index

Name Index